The
WINE
BOOK

James Wagenvoord

New York **quick fox** London

Introduction

The subject is *wine*. It adds taste and character to cooking, is superb in a number of unique mixed drinks, is unmatched on its own, and has a distinctive role in social and cultural history.

This book is an attempt to give dimension and meaning to your wine experience. The recipes for individual drinks and foods are proven and easy to follow. The tips on storage, uncorking, and serving and the sections on wines of the world are intended to broaden your understanding and enhance your enjoyment without self-consciousness.

Wine is not a cult experience. Yet often the language used to explain and instruct on the upper levels of the wine industry hierarchy smacks of the voices of fashion insiders. What seems to get lost in the avalanche of adjectives and superlatives is the fact that a good bottle of wine is terrific, that a well-made wine sauce can make an ordinary chicken or beef brisket a memorable dining experience, and that there are times when a Spritzer, or a French 75, or a well-blended punch provide some of life's more pleasant and relaxing moments. That is what this book is about.

Several people have been instrumental in the making of this book. The research was coordinated by Megan Marshack, who with Ted Stevenson drafted major portions of the text. A special thanks must also go to Mark Gabor and Fiona St. Aubyn for expert insights into the drink and food recipes.

Drinks & Recipes

Aperitifs: Sherry

Sherry Spritzer

8-oz. old-fashioned glass
4 oz. dry sherry
club soda
lemon peel strip

Pour sherry over crushed ice. Add equal
amount of soda. Add lemon twist.
(Note: This drink can be made using medium and sweet sherries.)

Caballero Cocktail

4-oz. whiskey-sour glass, chilled
1½ oz. dry sherry
1½ oz. dry vermouth
1 dash orange bitters

Combine ingredients in mixing container
with crushed ice. Stir vigorously. Strain
into glass.

Sherry Iced Coffee

4 6-oz. whiskey glasses, chilled
6 oz. sweet sherry, chilled
8 oz. black coffee, chilled
1 tsp. superfine sugar
2 oz. heavy cream
4 Tbsp. whipped cream
nutmeg

Place sherry, coffee, sugar, and cream in
mixing container with ice cubes. Stir vigorously. Strain into glasses. Top with
whipped cream and sprinkle with nutmeg.

Aperitifs: Sherry

Sherry Sunrise

2 5-oz. old-fashioned glasses, chilled
2 oz. dry or medium-dry sherry
2 oz. fresh orange juice, strained
1 tsp. superfine sugar

Add ingredients to shaker with ice cubes.
Shake vigorously. Strain into glasses.

Merry Widow

4-oz. old-fashioned glass
1½ oz. sherry
1½ oz. sweet vermouth
lemon peel strip

Combine liquids in mixing container.
Add ice cubes.
Stir lightly,
then strain into the glass.
Add lemon twist.

Silverado

2 6-oz. sherry glasses, chilled
blender jar, chilled
4 oz. dry sherry, chilled
½ tsp. fresh lemon juice, strained
½ tsp. superfine sugar
1 egg white

Blend ingredients at high speed until
smooth. Stir rapidly with ice cubes in
mixing container. Strain into glasses.

Aperitifs: Vermouth

Golden Calf

2 6-oz. sherry glasses, chilled
blender jar, chilled
4 oz. medium-sweet sherry, chilled
3 oz. milk
1 egg yolk

Blend ingredients at high speed until smooth. Stir with ice cubes in mixing container. Strain into glasses.

Coronation

3-oz. cocktail glass
1½ oz. medium sherry
1 oz. dry vermouth
3 dashes orange bitters
2 dashes maraschino liqueur

Combine ingredients in mixing container with ice cubes. Stir, then strain into glass.

Aperitifs: Vermouth

Vermouth Cassis

8-oz. wine glass
4 oz. dry vermouth
lemon peel strip
1½ tsp. creme de cassis
cold club soda

Pour vermouth into glass and add ice cubes. Twist lemon peel over glass and drop in. Add the cassis. Fill glass with soda and stir lightly.

Aperitifs: Vermouth

Americano

8-oz. wine glass
4 oz. sweet vermouth
1½ oz. Campari
orange peel strip
club soda

Pour vermouth and bitters into wine glass.
Twist orange peel over glass, rub around
rim, and drop in. Add ice cubes, fill with
soda, and stir lightly.

Trocadero

3-oz. cocktail glass
1 oz. dry vermouth
1 oz. sweet vermouth
1 dash grenadine
1 dash orange bitters

Shake ingredients in mixing
container half-filled with ice.
Strain, and serve plain.

Brazil

3-oz. cocktail glass
1 oz. dry vermouth
1 oz. sherry
1 dash Pernod
1 dash Angostura bitters
lemon peel strip

Add liquid ingredients to crushed ice in
mixing container. Stir and strain into glass.
Twist lemon peel and drop in.

Aperitifs: Vermouth

Cherry Mixture

3-oz. cocktail glass
1 oz. sweet vermouth
1 oz. dry vermouth
1 dash Angostura bitters
1 dash maraschino liqueur
1 cherry

Add liquid ingredients to crushed ice in mixing container. Stir and strain into glass. Add cherry.

Hot Summer

8-oz. highball glass
1½ oz. rye whiskey
1 oz. sweet vermouth
ginger beer
1 cherry
1 mint leaf
1 lemon slice

Add whiskey and vermouth to ice-filled glass. Fill with ginger beer and decorate with cherry, mint, and lemon.

Dry Vermouth Cocktail

3-oz. cocktail glass
2 oz. dry vermouth
2 dashes orange bitters
2 drops Angostura bitters
olive
lemon peel strip

Add liquid ingredients to crushed ice in mixing container. Stir and strain. Add olive and lemon twist.

Aperitifs: Dubonnet

Matriarch

3-oz. cocktail glass
2½ oz. dry vermouth
1 dash curacao
1 dash essence of mint
orange peel strip

Pour liquid ingredients into mixing container half-filled with ice.
Stir well. Strain into glass,
twist orange peel, and drop in.

Dubonnet

Ambrosia

10-oz. collins glass
2 oz. Dubonnet
1 lump sugar
2 dashes bitters
champagne
lemon peel strip

Stir liquids with several ice cubes, adding champagne last to fill glass. Twist lemon peel and drop in.

Appetizer

5-oz. old-fashioned glass
2 oz. Dubonnet
2 oz. fresh orange juice

Shake ingredients well with crushed ice in mixing container. Strain, serve plain.

Aperitifs: Dubonnet

Dubonnet Cocktail

4 oz. cocktail glass, chilled
2 oz. red Dubonnet
1 oz. gin
1 dash orange bitters
orange peel strip

Combine liquids with ice cubes in mixing container. Stir lightly and strain into cocktail glass. Twist orange peel, rub around rim of glass, but do not drop in.

Phoebe

4-oz. cocktail glass
1½ oz. Dubonnet
1½ oz. brandy
1 dash absinthe

Stir with crushed ice in mixing container. Strain, serve plain.

Aviation

4-oz. cocktail glass
1½ oz. Dubonnet
1½ oz. dry sherry
orange peel strip

Shake liquids with crushed ice in mixing container. Strain and serve with orange peel twist.

Champagne

Champagne Cocktail

champagne glass, chilled
1 sugar cube
Angostura bitters
dry champagne, chilled
lemon peel strip
1 tsp. brandy (optional)

Saturate sugar with bitters in glass. Add champagne and lemon twist. If using brandy, float it on top of champagne by pouring in very slowly.

Dinah's Cocktail

12-oz. collins glass
2 oz. Cognac
very dry champagne, chilled
lemon peel strip

Pour cognac over ice cubes. Fill glass to top with champagne. Stir lightly and add lemon twist.

French 75

8-oz. wine glass, chilled
3 oz. gin
1½ oz. fresh lemon juice, strained
1 egg white
1 Tbsp. heavy cream
1½ tsp. superfine sugar
3 oz. champagne, chilled

Combine gin, lemon juice, egg white, cream, and sugar in mixing container. Shake vigorously for four to five seconds. Strain into glass and fill with champagne, pouring gently.

Champagne

Maxim's Champagne Cocktail

champagne glass, chilled
dry champagne, chilled
2 brandied cherries
1 tsp. superfine sugar

Mix ingredients together. Stir very gently
to dissolve sugar.

Champagne

Mimosa

10-oz. collins glass, chilled
champagne
fresh orange juice, strained

Fill glass with crushed ice. Pour in equal
parts champagne and juice.

Black Velvet

large straight glass or stein
dry champagne, chilled
Guinness stout, chilled

Fill glass with equal parts champagne
and stout.

Peach Velvet

champagne glass, chilled
wedge-shaped slice fresh peach
dry champagne, chilled
½ tsp. peach brandy

Place peach in glass and fill with champagne. Top with peach brandy.

Fiona's Flameout

10-oz. highball glass
dry champagne
1 oz. Cointreau
1 oz. Cognac
1 oz. Benedictine
1 oz. vodka
1 oz. lime juice

Combine last five ingredients in mixing
container with crushed ice. Shake well,
strain into glass. Fill glass with champagne.

Wine: Miscellaneous

Wine Coolers

12-oz. collins glass
wine of choice
1 oz. fruit liqueur of choice
1 tsp. sugar (omit with port or sherry)
lemon peel strip
mint sprig

Fill glass with crushed ice. Add liqueur,
sugar, and fill glass with chosen wine.
Stir with long spoon until glass frosts.
Add lemon twist, garnish with mint.

Spritzer

12-oz. collins glass
wine of choice (usually dry white)
club soda
lemon peel strip

Fill glass with ice. Pour wine to within one
inch from rim of glass. Top with soda. Add
lemon twist.

Claret Lemonade

12 oz. collins glass
1½ tsp. superfine sugar
juice from 1 lemon, strained
8 oz. claret wine, chilled
club soda
slice of lemon

Place sugar and lemon juice in glass. Stir
to dissolve sugar. Fill glass halfway with
crushed ice, then fill nearly to the rim
with claret. Top with club soda. Garnish
with lemon slice. Serve with straw.

Cups

Bacchus Cup

4 wine or punch glasses, chilled
1 bottle champagne, chilled
4 oz. brandy
4 oz. sweet liqueur of choice
2 oz. superfine sugar
½ sliced cucumber, unpeeled
1 bottle (32 oz.) club soda, chilled

When ready to serve, mix all ingredients together in large pitcher or bowl. Add ice cubes.

Moselle or Muscadet Cup

4 wine or punch glasses, chilled
1 bottle Moselle or Muscadet, chilled
2 oz. curaçao
2 oz. Benedictine
2 oz. brandy
2 cups mixed fresh fruit (optional)

Mix all ingredients except soda with ice cubes in large pitcher or bowl. Stir until well chilled. Add soda just before serving.

Cups

Sauternes Cup

4 wine or punch glasses, chilled
1 bottle Sauternes, chilled
4 oz. brandy
4 oz. Cointreau
4 oz. Grand Marnier
1 cup mixed fresh fruit juice of choice
6 oz. club soda, chilled

Combine Sauternes, brandy, Cointreau, Grand Marnier, and fruit in large pitcher or bowl. Refrigerate at least one hour. Just before serving, add soda and ice.

Cups

Chablis Cup

4 wine or punch glasses, chilled
1 lemon
1 cup superfine sugar
1 bottle Chablis, chilled
1 bottle (32 oz.) club soda, chilled

Peel lemon rind and reserve. Thinly slice
rest of lemon. In large bowl, dissolve sugar
in wine and add lemon slices. When ready
to serve, mix with soda and ice. Garnish
each glass with twist of lemon peel.

Rhine Wine Cup

4 wine or punch glasses, chilled
1 bottle Rhine wine, chilled
2 oz. curaçao (optional)
1 bottle (32 oz.) club soda, chilled
orange or lemon slices
mint sprigs

When ready to serve, combine liquids
with ice. Add orange or lemon slices.
Stir lightly. Garnish glasses with mint
sprigs. If stronger mixture is desired, use
two bottles of wine to one of soda.
(Note: A Peach Cup variation calls for two
large, skinned peaches cut into small pieces
Add to the mixture, along with two Tbsp.
superfine sugar.)

Cups

Celery Cup

4 wine or punch glasses, chilled
1 large bunch celery
2 to 3 Tbsp. superfine sugar
½ cup light rum
½ cup water
1 bottle Moselle wine, chilled

Trim celery leaves and reserve. Thinly slice stalks into a bowl. Sprinkle with sugar and stir in rum and water. Cover bowl and refrigerate one to two hours. Strain, discarding celery bits. Pour mixture into pitcher and add ice and wine. Mix well and pour into glasses. Garnish with celery leaves.

Badminton Cup

4 wine or punch glasses, chilled
1 bottle claret, chilled
½ medium cucumber, sliced
2 tsp. superfine sugar
2 oz. curacao
juice of 1 lemon
1 bottle (32 oz.) club soda, chilled
nutmeg

Pour wine over the cucumber and sugar. Stir until sugar dissolves. Add curaçao, lemon juice, ice, and soda. Serve with a sprinkle of nutmeg.

Eggnogs

Sherry, Port, Brandy, or Rum Eggnog

6 to 8 10-oz. goblets, chilled
1 bottle sherry, port, brandy, or rum
1 qt. milk or light cream
8 eggs
8 tsp. superfine sugar
nutmeg

Vigorously mix all ingredients except
nutmeg in a large bowl until smooth and
creamy. A blender can also be used at low
speed. Refrigerate until chilled. Top each
serving with sprinkle of nutmeg.
(*Note:* A variation known as Baltimore
Eggnog calles for two cups brandy and
two cups rum in place of spirits listed
above.)

Eggnogs

McGregor's Eggnog

6 to 8 10-oz. goblets, chilled
2 cups dry sherry
1 cup Cognac
1 cup rum
2 Tbsp. superfine sugar
6 eggs
1 qt. milk
nutmeg

Mix all ingredients except nutmeg in
large bowl until creamy and smooth. A
blender can also be used at low speed.
Refrigerate until chilled. Pour into goblets.
Sprinkle with nutmeg.

Flips

General Harrisons Eggnog

6 10-oz. collins glasses, chilled
6 eggs
2 Tbsp. confectioner's sugar
claret
nutmeg

Combine eggs and sugar with ice cubes in mixing glass. Shake vigorously and divide into equal portions in the glasses. Fill each glass with the claret. Stir. Sprinkle with nutmeg.

Sherry Flip

6-oz. whiskey-sour glass, chilled
1 egg
1 tsp. superfine sugar
3 oz. medium sherry
nutmeg

Combine egg, sugar, and sherry with ice cubes in a mixing glass. Shake vigorously for four to five seconds. Strain into glass. Sprinkle with nutmeg.
(*Note:* Other flips can be made by substituting any of the following for the sherry—port, Madeira, Marsala, brandy, whiskey, light rum, gin, or vodka.)

Punches

Pineapple Punch

4 to 6 punch glasses, chilled
1 fresh or medium-sized can pineapple
2 cups dry red wine
2 cups dry white wine
2 cups port
2 oz. superfine sugar
1 bottle sparkling wine of choice
mint sprigs

Cut pineapple into bite-sized chunks.
Combine with red and white wines, port,
and sugar. Stir lightly until sugar dissolves.
Chill for one or more hours. When ready
to serve, add ice cubes and sparkling wine.
Garnish with mint sprigs.

Fish House Punch

4 to 6 punch glasses, chilled
1 cup superfine sugar
1 pt. fresh lemon juice
1 qt. light or dark rum
1 pt. Cognac
½ cup peach brandy
1 qt. water
1 cup mixed fresh fruit (optional)

Combine sugar and lemon juice in
large bowl. Mix until sugar dissolves.
Add rum, Cognac, brandy, and water.
Stir. Allow mixture to stand at room
temperature for two hours, stirring
periodically. Refrigerate for one hour.
Just before serving, add ice cubes and
fruit.

Punches

Champagne Punch

4 to 6 punch glasses, chilled
2 bottles champagne, chilled
3 oz. brandy
1 oz. maraschino liqueur
1 oz. curaçao
1 dash yellow chartreuse
2 bottles (32 oz.) club soda, chilled
juice of 4 lemons
sugar (optional)
1 cup fresh mixed fruit

When ready to serve, mix all ingredients together in large punch bowl. Add ice cubes and sugar to taste.

Tea Punch

4 to 6 punch glasses, chilled
3 Tbsp. tea leaves of choice
1 bottle sweet white wine of choice, chilled
½ cup lemon juice
1 orange, sliced
1 lemon, sliced
¾ lb. whole strawberries or cherries
1 medium-sized can pineapple chunks

Pour one quart boiling water over tea leaves and let steep for five minutes. Strain, discard leaves. Add wine and lemon juice to tea. Pour over ice cubes in large punch bowl. Add fruit.

Punches

Claret Punch

4 to 6 punch glasses, chilled
1 bottle claret, chilled
6 oz. sherry
2 oz. curacao
1 bottle (32 oz.) club soda
thinly-sliced cucumber
thinly-sliced rind of 1 lemon
sugar to taste

When ready to serve, pour liquids over ice in large punch bowl. Garnish punch with cucumber slices and lemon rind. Add sugar if desired.

Brandy Punch

6 8-oz. goblets, chilled
1 fifth brandy
1 tsp. grenadine
1 tsp. maraschino liqueur
1 bottle (32 oz.) club soda
2 cups mixed fresh fruit
mint sprigs

Combine all ingredients with ice in chilled punch bowl. Stir lightly. Ladle into mint-garnished goblets.

White Christmas Punch

4 to 6 punch glasses, chilled
2 bottles champagne, chilled
1 cup vodka
½ cup Cointreau
½ cup kirsch
12 strips cucumber rind

Combine all ingredients. Pour over a quart-sized ice block in a large bowl. Garnish punch with cucumber strips.

Punches

Anne's Sligo Sangria

4 to 6 punch glasses, chilled
8 oz. water
½ cup superfine sugar
1 tsp. cinnamon
2 oranges, sliced
1 lemon and/or lime, sliced
1 bottle medium-dry red wine
other fresh fruit (optional)
3 oz. brandy (optional)

Combine water, sugar, and cinnamon in saucepan. Cook over moderate heat until ingredients dissolve into a syrup. Slice citrus fruit, put into bowl, and add syrup mixture. Allow to stand for four or more hours at room temperature.

Place ice cubes in large pitcher. Add 2/3 cup syrup, citrus slices, and wine to pitcher. If desired, add fresh fruit and brandy. Stir until pitcher is frosted.
(Note: Medium-dry white wine can also be used to make sangria.)

Syllabub

3 to 4 wine or punch glasses, chilled
1 bottle medium dry sherry, chilled
2 oz. brandy
1 qt. light cream
juice of 2 oranges
rind of 2 oranges, grated
½ cup superfine sugar
1 tsp. orange water (optional)

Mix all ingredients in large bowl. Pour approximately three cups at a time into blender and mix on low speed until foamy. Pour mixture over ice cubes in large punch bowl. Continue blending batches as needed.

31

Hot Wine Drinks

Port Bishop

4 to 6 mugs or punch cups, warmed
1½ bottles port
2 cups boiling water
2 oranges
2 oz. lump sugar
1 stick cinnamon
24 cloves
freshly grated nutmeg

Spike one orange all around with cloves.
Bake at 350° until a rich brown. Rub
sugar on rind of second orange and place in
a bowl, adding the juice of the orange.
Thickly slice the baked orange and add
to bowl, along with cinnamon. Heat port
almost to boiling. Add port and water to
mixture. When served in cups, sprinkle
with nutmeg.
(*Note:* For a variation known as Archbishop,
substitute claret for the port.)

Mulled Wine

4 to 6 mugs or punch cups, warmed
1 bottle port, claret, or Burgundy
2 oz. brandy (optional)
1 cup boiling water
½ cup superfine sugar
rind of ½ lemon, cut in strips
1 stick cinnamon
6 cloves
freshly grated nutmeg

Simmer all ingredients except wine and
nutmeg for 10 to 15 minutes. Warm wine
separately; do not allow to boil. Strain
first mixture, discarding residue. Combine
with wine and brandy. Serve piping hot,
sprinkled with nutmeg.

Hot Wine Drinks

Pope's Posset

4 to 6 mugs or punch cups, warmed
1 bottle medium sherry
2 cups water
6 Tbsp. sugar
1¼ almonds, blanched

Crush almonds with a little water to make a smooth, buttery paste. Mix thoroughly with two cups of water. Bring quickly to boil, then simmer two minutes. In a separate saucepan, bring sherry and sugar almost to boiling. Combine with almond mixture in warmed punch bowl. Serve immediately.

Christmas Wassail

4 to 6 mugs or punch cups, warmed
1 tsp. cinnamon
½ tsp. ground ginger
½ tsp. allspice
¼ tsp. ground cloves
¼ tsp. nutmeg
¼ cup water
2 bottles dry red or white wine
2 cups superfine sugar
7 eggs, separated
7 baked apples

Stir spices into boiling water and simmer for 30 seconds. Add wine to saucepan and heat almost to boiling. Add sugar and stir until dissolved. Beat egg yolks until lemon-colored. Beat egg whites until smooth and creamy. Fold yolks into whites lightly in large punch bowl. Pour wine-and-spice mixture gently into punch bowl. Whip until frothy. Float hot baked apples on top.

Hot Wine Drinks

Glögg

4 to 6 mugs or punch cups, warmed
1 bottle red Bordeaux
1 bottle port or sweet sherry
2 cups Cognac
1 cup sugar
1 cup seedless raisins
16 cloves
2 sticks cinnamon
1 cup whole blanched almonds

Stir all ingredients over low heat until
sugar dissolves. Do not boil. Simmer over
lowest heat for 15 minutes. Serve in
heated, flameproof silver bowl.
Ignite mixture, then ladle into
cups. Spoon equal amounts of raisins and almonds into each serving.

Hot Wine Drinks

Hot Wine Drinks

Spanish Tisane

3 to 4 mugs or punch cups, warmed
2 cups Malaga wine
1 cup tart orange marmalade
6 cups boiling water
juice of lemon or lime (optional)

Simmer all ingredients for ½ hour or
until all traces of marmalade dissolve.
Lemon or lime juice can be added to
taste if mixture is too sweet.

Negus

3 to 4 mugs or punch cups, warmed
6 sugar cubes
1½ Tbsp. lemon extract
3 cups boiling water
1 bottle port or sherry
nutmeg

Add sugar and lemon extract to boiling
water. When sugar dissolves, add port or
sherry and bring to simmer. Serve
sprinkled with nutmeg.

Sherry Posset

4 to 6 mugs or punch cups, warmed
1 bottle medium sherry
2 cups light ale
4 cups milk
¾ cup sugar
nutmeg

Scald milk in a saucepan. In another pan,
heat sherry and ale. Add sugar and stir
until dissolved. When approaching boiling

Hot Wine Drinks

point, transfer to milk pot, stirring gently.
Sprinkle with nutmeg and serve.
(*Note:* A variation known as Sack Posset
calls for the addition of three egg yolks,
whipped smooth, then added to the complete mixture just before serving.)

Chill Killer

4 to 6 mugs or punch cups, warmed
1½ cups sugar
6 cups boiling water
3 cups sherry
1½ cups rum
¼ cup brandy
¾ cup stout
juice of 3 lemons
3 lemon rinds, grated

Dissolve sugar in boiling water. Add other
ingredients, carefully stirring each one in.
Heat and stir until mixture starts to foam.
Serve immediately.

Spiced Hot Kir

3 to 4 mugs or punch cups, warmed
1 bottle dry white wine
1 cup crème de cassis
1 lemon, thinly sliced
1 lemon rind, cut in strips
8 whole allspice
4 large sticks of cinnamon

Combine all ingredients except lemon
strips and simmer 10 to 12 minutes.
Ladle through a strainer into the cups.
Garnish each with a lemon twist.

Brandy Drinks

Brandy and Bitters

10-oz. highball glass
1½ oz. brandy
club soda
3 dashes Angostura bitters
lemon peel strip

Combine ingredients in glass, adding soda
and ice cubes last. Stir. Add twist of lemon.

Brandy Cocktail

12-oz. highball or collins glass
1 oz. brandy
1 oz. curaçao
1 tsp. ginger syrup (optional)
2 tsp. orange bitters

Combine ingredients in mixing container
half-filled with crushed ice. Shake five
seconds. Strain into glass.

Sensation

12-oz. collins or highball glass
2 oz. brandy
juice of 1 orange, strained
juice of ½ lemon, strained
1 Tbsp. raspberry syrup
½ slice pineapple
sugar to taste
club soda

Combine all ingredients with ice in glass.
Stir. Top with club soda.

Brandy Drinks

Brandy Cruster

4-oz. stemmed cocktail glass
1½ oz. brandy
½ oz. curaçao
1½ oz. orange juice
1 Tbsp. fine sugar

Dip rim of glass into orange juice, then into sugar to create crust. Combine liquids in mixing container half-filled with ice. Shake vigorously. Strain into glass.

Brandy Smash

5-oz. champagne glass, chilled
mint sprigs
3 oz. brandy
½ tsp. sugar
club soda
berries or other fresh fruit (optional)

Crush mint and place on top of glass filled with crushed ice. Add brandy and sugar. Stir. Fill glass with squirt of club soda. If desired, add fruit.

Brandy Rickey

8-oz. highball glass
1½ oz. brandy
club soda
juice of ½ lime
rind of ½ lime, thinly sliced

Add brandy, juice, and rind to glass with ice. Fill with soda. Stir.

Brandy Drinks

Sevilla Special

4-oz. cocktail glass
1 oz. brandy
1 oz. light rum
1 oz. fresh lemon juice
1 tsp. superfine sugar

Combine ingredients in mixing container half-filled with crushed ice. Shake for five seconds and strain.

8-oz. highball glass
1½ oz. brandy
1½ oz. light rum
juice of ½ lime
sugar to taste
1 tsp. curaçao
club soda

Combine ingredients except soda in mixing container half-filled with ice. Shake well. Strain. Fill glass with soda. Stir.

Whip

5-oz. old-fashioned glass
1½ oz. brandy
1 oz. sweet vermouth
1 oz. dry vermouth
1 Tbsp. curaçao
1 tsp. Pernod

Combine all ingredients in mixing container half-filled with ice. Shake and strain.

Hot Brandy Drinks

Hot Toddy

4 to 6 mugs or punch cups, warmed
1 lemon
20 cloves
1 qt. brandy, whiskey, bourbon, or rum
2 qts. boiling water
sugar to taste
cinnamon

Spike lemon with cloves, then cut into four
to six slices. Add lemon slices and liquor
to heated bowl. Pour in boiling water. Add
sugar to desired sweetness. Stir mixture.
Ladle one lemon slice into each cup and
sprinkle each serving with cinnamon.

Farmer's Bishop

4 to 6 mugs or punch cups, warmed
1 bottle apple brandy
2 qts. apple cider
5 oranges
75 to 100 whole cloves
4 to 6 long cinnamon sticks

Spike the oranges with 15 to 20 cloves and
bake for 25 minutes at 300°. Heat the
brandy and cider in separate saucepans
almost to boiling. In a metal punch bowl
or pot, place the oranges and add the hot
brandy. Ignite. After a minute or so, dowse
the blue flame with hot cider. Ladle hot
mixture into mugs and garnish each with a
cinnamon stick.

Hot Brandy Drinks

Café Brûlot

6 8-oz. cups or mugs, warmed
1½ cups brandy or Cognac
3 oz. curaçao
1 qt. strong black coffee
1 orange rind, cut in thin strips
1 lemon rind, cut in thin strips
2 cinnamon sticks, halved lengthwise
12 cloves
8 sugar cubes

Combine all ingredients except coffee in a chafing dish. Over gentle heat, stir and mash mixture for several minutes until sugar dissolves. When very hot, carefully ignite and let mixture burn for up to one minute. Gradually add coffee until flames go out. Ladle into cups or mugs.

Café Royal

6 6-oz. old-fashioned glasses
1½ cups brandy or Cognac
12 lemon peel strips
6 cups strong black coffee
superfine sugar
3 cinnamon sticks

Rub lemon peel around the rim of each glass. Dip rim of each glass into sugar. Twist remaining lemon peels over each glass and drop in. Add half a cinnamon stick to each glass. Heat brandy or Cognac in chafing dish. Before pouring, place a small metal spoon in each glass to prevent cracking. Ladle the hot liquid into each glass, ignite, and let burn for up to one minute. Add hot coffee and serve.

Sauces

Red Wine Gravy

4 Tbsps. butter
4 Tbsp. flour
½ cup dry red wine
1½ cups beef bouillon
salt and pepper

Mix butter and flour in skillet and stir
until brown. Add wine and bouillon
gradually, stirring until smooth and thick.
Season to taste. Serve with red meats.
Yields 2 cups.

Tartar Sauce with White Wine

1 cup mayonnaise
3 Tbsp. dry white wine
1 Tbsp. dill pickles, minced
1 Tbsp. capers, minced
1 Tbsp. olives, minced
1 Tbsp. parsley, chopped

Mix all ingredients.
Serve over fish, shellfish, raw vegetables.
Yields 1¼ cups.

Hollandaise Sauce with Sauternes

1½ cups butter
6 egg yolks, beaten lightly
1 Tbsp. boiling water
¼ cup Sauternes
salt

Heat water in bottom part of double boiler
but do not boil. Melt butter in top pan and
beat in egg yolks one at a time until
blended. Add boiling water. Add wine a

Sauces

little bit at a time, stirring briskly. Remove
from heat and season.
Serve over fish, green vegetables, eggs
Benedict.
Yields 2 cups.

Red Wine Sauce

1 small onion, chopped
2 cloves garlic, crushed
1 Tbsp. butter
3 Tbsp. flour
2 cups red wine
4 small potatoes, peeled and chopped
1 tsp. tomato purée
1½ Tbsp. sweet sherry or Madeira
1 bay leaf
salt and pepper

Sauté onion and garlic in butter. Mix in
flour. Add wine and bring to a boil. Add
the remaining ingredients. Cover the pan,
turn down heat, and simmer for 15 minutes. Serve with game, red meat, pot roast.
Yields 3 cups

Sauce with Capers

1 cup chicken stock
½ cup dry white wine
1 Tbsp. butter
1 Tbsp. flour
2 Tbsp. capers
1 Tbsp. caper juice
½ tsp. salt
¼ tsp. pepper
4 Tbsp. sour cream

Combine chicken stock and wine and boil
until reduced by one-third. Add butter and
flour, stirring over low heat until thickened.
Add capers, liquid, and seasoning. Remove
from heat and add sour cream.
Serve with chicken, pork, veal, fish, and
green vegetables.
Yields 2 cups.

Chicken and Eggs

Continental Eggs

3 Tbsp. butter
6 hard-cooked eggs, chopped
½ cup cooked shrimp
½ tsp. dry mustard
2 Tbsp. fino sherry
1 Tbsp. chopped parsley
1 cup cream
½ tsp. salt
dash of cayenne
paprika
toast triangles

Melt butter and add other ingredients, one by one. Gently stir over low heat until the mixture begins to simmer. While hot, spoon over toast triangles and dust with paprika.
Yields three servings.

Coq au Vin

2 Tbsp. olive oil
1 or 2 cloves of garlic, crushed
6 small white onions, chopped
1 chicken, cut into serving pieces
2 cups dry red wine
2 bay leaves
bouquet garni
salt and pepper
4 Tbsp. butter
2 Tbsp. flour
1/3 lb. button mushrooms, peeled

Heat olive oil. Sauté garlic and onions briefly, then add chicken giblets and wing tips. After browning, add wine, bay leaves, and bouquet garni. Salt and pepper to taste. Bring to a boil. Lower heat, cover and simmer for two hours.
   In the meantime, sauté chicken pieces

Chicken and Eggs

in three tablespoons butter. Place in a casserole dish. Combine flour and remaining tablespoon butter.

When the stock is cooked, reserve onions with slotted spoon. Add onions and mushrooms to casserole. Strain remaining stock into butter and flour mixture. Stir until thickened, then pour over chicken. This can be prepared in advance. Before serving, cover casserole and heat in a 325° oven for 30 minutes. Yields four servings.

Ambrosia Chicken Salad

2 cups cooked chicken, chopped
1 cup seedless white grapes
2 large oranges, sliced
1 cup semi-sweet white wine
6 to 8 Tbsp. peanut or vegetable oil
1 cup celery, chopped
¼ cup scallions, finely chopped
¼ cup blanched almonds, sliced
4 Tbsp. butter
½ tsp. curry powder
lettuce

Put chicken and grapes in a medium-sized dish. Place orange slices on top and add wine. Refrigerate a minimum of two hours.

Just before serving, pour wine marinade into a saucepan and heat until reduced to three tablespoons. Make a French dressing by combining the reduced wine with the oil. Sauté almonds, celery, and scallions in butter. Mix chicken, fruit, dressing, nuts, and scallions. Sprinkle with curry powder. Chill for ten minutes. Serve on a bed of lettuce. Yields four servings.

Meat

Lamb Chops Provençal

6 medium-sized lamb chops
2 medium-sized onions, chopped
3 cloves garlic, sliced
4 Tbsp. olive oil
1 lb. tomatoes, chopped (save juice)
1½ Tbsp. tomato purée
salt and pepper
1 cup dry white wine
fresh basil

Fry lamb chops and keep warm in oven.
Sauté onion and garlic in olive oil until
tender. Add tomatoes and their juice and
tomato purée to pan. Add seasonings and
wine and bring to a boil. Cook over
medium flame for ten minutes. Place chops
in serving dish with tomatoes arranged
around them. Garnish with basil.
Yields three to four servings.

Steak au Poivre

2½ Tbsp. cracked pepper
A 2½-lb. steak, 1-inch thick
1½ Tbsp. vegetable oil
5 Tbsp. butter
2 Tbsp. scallions, finely chopped
½ cup beef stock
1/3 cup Cognac

Press cracked pepper into both sides of the
steak with your hands. Cover with waxed
paper and let stand for 1½ hours.
   Sauté steak in oil and one tablespoon
butter. Sprinkle with salt and remove to a
hot platter. Cook scallions in one table-

Meat

spoon butter in same skillet. Add stock and boil rapidly while scraping the pan. Pour in Cognac and boil for about one minute. Remove from stove and add three tablespoons butter, a teaspoon at a time. Pour sauce over steak, add more pepper if desired, and serve.
Yields four servings.

Escalopes de Veau au Champagne

4 Tbsp. clarified butter
1 lb. veal scallops
2 Tbsp. scallions, minced
1 cup fresh mushrooms, sliced
1 cup extra-dry champagne
1 cup light cream
½ tsp. freshly grated nutmeg
salt and pepper
4 Tbsp. salted butter, softened

In a large saucepan, gently heat clarified butter. Brown veal for about two minutes on each side. Add scallions and mushrooms and cook two minutes. Add champagne, turn heat to high and reduce. Add cream, nutmeg, salt and pepper. Reduce heat and simmer four minutes. Remove veal and mushrooms to serving dish. In the same saucepan, over high heat, finish sauce by adding softened butter. Pour over veal and serve.
Yields two servings.
(*Note:* To clarify butter, melt seven tablespoons butter. Skim it with a spoon. Carefully pour off the clear liquid. Discard the milky sediment at the bottom of the pan. Clarified butter keeps for one month if refrigerated.)

49

Fish and Shell Fish

Camarones o Gambas en Salsa de Sherry

¼ cup olive oil
4 Tbsp. butter
1 medium-sized onion, thinly sliced
3 garlic cloves, grated
1 bay leaf
36 raw shrimp, peeled, washed, and deveined
salt and freshly ground pepper
6 Tbsp. fresh parsley, finely chopped
¾ cup fino sherry

Heat olive oil and butter in a large skillet.
Add onion, garlic, and bay leaf and cook
until brown. Stir in shrimp and coat with
oil. Add seasonings, parsley, and sherry.
Cook until shrimp are bright pink, about
five to eight minutes. Remove bay leaf.
Serve with chilled fino or amontillado
sherry.
Yields six servings.

Fillets of Sole with White Wine

1 cup semi-sweet white wine
2 cups seedless white grapes
6 fillets of sole or flounder
½ cup fish stock
1 Tbsp. lemon juice   2 Tbsp. flour
2 Tbsp. shallots, sliced   2 Tbsp. butter
1 tsp. thyme   ½ cup cream
salt and pepper   12 shrimp, cooked

Heat wine in saucepan and add grapes,
cooking for five minutes. Set grapes aside.
Place fillets in larger saucepan, add wine
in which grapes were cooked, fish stock,

Fish and Shell Fish

lemon juice, shallots, and seasonings.
Simmer for five minutes. Reduce sauce
by half. Combine flour and butter. Add
to sauce and stir constantly for three
minutes. Add cream and bring to a boil.
Pour over fillets. Place grapes around the
fillets and shrimp on top. Brown lightly
under broiler.
Yields six servings.

Fillets of Sole with Champagne

12 large fillets of sole
2 cups brut champagne
1 small finely chopped onion
7 oz. butter
salt and freshly ground pepper
6 Tbsp. heavy cream
4 egg yolks

Place the fillets in a frying pan and cover
with champagne. Add onion, one tablespoon butter, and salt and pepper. Bring
to a boil slowly, then reduce heat, and
simmer for six to eight minutes. Remove
fillets gently to a serving dish and place in
a warm oven.

Melt remaining butter. Add cream and
egg yolks. Beat with a wire whisk for five
minutes. Add enough of the cooking sauce
to form a creamy sauce. Heat the sauce,
but do not boil. Pour over the fillets and
serve.
Yields six servings.

Desserts

Mrs. Hill's Trifle with Sherry

1 cup sugar
½ tsp. salt
1 Tbsp. cornstarch
4 cups milk
8 egg yolks
2 tsp. vanilla extract
¾ cup plus 1 Tbsp. cream sherry
2 8-inch packaged sponge cakes
6 Tbsp. raspberry preserves
6 Tbsp. toasted slivered almonds
½ cup whipped cream

In a medium-heavy saucepan, combine sugar, salt, and cornstarch. Add the milk slowly, stirring constantly. Cook over medium heat, until mixture thickens. Turn up the heat and let the mixture boil briefly. Remove.

Beat the egg yolks. Stir a little of the hot mixture into yolks. Pour remaining milk mixture into yolks. Return the sauce to the pan and cook over medium heat, stirring constantly, until mixture reaches the boiling point. Remove from heat and blend in vanilla and one tablespoon sherry.

Strain the custard into a bowl. Refrigerate for several hours or overnight.

Split sponge cake layers horizontally. Place a layer of cake on a circular dessert plate. Sprinkle with sherry, spread with two tablespoons preserves, two tablespoons almonds, and one cup of custard. Repeat two more times. Cover with the final layer of cake and spread the remaining custard on top and decorate with cream.

Yields eight to ten servings.

Desserts

Champagne Sabayon with Strawberries

36 to 40 strawberries (about 1½ pints)
6 egg yolks
7 oz. (1 scant cup) sugar
2 cups brut champagne

Hull and wash strawberries. Divide into six portions.

In the top half of a double boiler, beat egg yolks and sugar to a creamy consistency. Gradually stir in the champagne. Place over hot water and cook, stirring constantly, until thick and creamy. Pour over strawberries and serve.
Yields six servings.

Champagne Sherbet

2 cups sugar
2½ cups water
juice of 4 large lemons
4 cups champagne
2 egg whites

Combine sugar and water. Cook until syrupy. Reserve four tablespoons. Combine lemon juice and remaining syrup. Gradually stir in all but about ¼ cup champagne. Strain through a fine sieve. Beat egg whites with four tablespoons syrup until stiff. Fold in the remaining champagne.

Combine the mixtures. Freeze until ready to serve.
Yields four servings.

Desserts

Sherry Colada Dessert

1¼ cups fino sherry
¾ cup dry white wine
2 cups crushed fresh pineapple
3 oz. fresh pineapple juice
1 Tbsp. lemon juice
6 small pineapple wedges

Combine all ingredients except pineapple wedges in a lidded jar. Marinate four hours in refrigerator. Spoon into chilled parfait glasses. Garnish with pineapple wedges.
Yields six servings.

Sherry Fondue

2 cups amontillado sherry
2 large cloves garlic, split
1 Tbsp. lemon juice
1 lb. Swiss Emmanthaler cheese, shredded
4 Tbsp. flour
freshly ground white pepper
paprika
crusty French or Italian bread, cut into
    cubes

Put garlic on long wooden skewers and place in wine. Heat sherry over moderate heat in fondue pot or double boiler. When wine is hot, add lemon juice. Remove garlic and discard. Toss cheese with flour. Gradually add cheese in small amounts to the wine, stirring constantly with a wooden spoon.

When all the cheese has melted, add pepper and a dash of paprika. Keep hot over fondue or other burner.

Spear bread with fondue forks, dunk, and swirl to cover with fondue.
Yields four servings.

Wine:
Varieties,
Care
&
Serving

The grape vine is cultivated wherever the climate permits it, with the result that there is an infinite variety in the wines that find their way to market. But the great wine-producing areas have more than just adequate sunshine. The second section of *The Wine Book* describes these areas, with a profile of each country—including maps and photos—and details of its major wines. In addition, there is straight-forward, accessible information on the care and storage of wine as well as on how best to serve it. The aim of this book is to allow you to develop your enjoyment of and pleasure in the nectar of the Gods as fully as possible.

How Wine Is Made

How Wine Is Made

Winemaking begins with the grape harvest and deciding when to pick the grapes is part of the vintner's art. Nowadays, the time of picking is determined by scientific testing of both sugar and acid content of the juice, but the actual decision to pick the grapes is still a bit of a human gamble—possible improvement of the grape is balanced against potential weather damage or other spoilage.

CRUSHING Once picked, the grapes are transported quickly and carefully to the winery, and the actual processing begins with destemming and crushing. The mass of juice and grape solids resulting from the crushing is called "must." The must is immediately treated with sulfur dioxide, a gas that acts as a sterilizer, killing all the potentially harmful microorganisms without harming the natural wine years that live on the grape skins.

PRESSING Pressing, as the name suggests, is the separation of the juice from the solid grape residues (skins, stems, and seeds) which is known as "pomace" after the pressing. The quality of the juice depends on the degree that the must is pressed in extracting the juice. Some premium wines are made using only the free-run juice. Juice from later pressings is used for blending lesser wines. White wines, which are often made from red-skinned grapes, are pressed promptly after crushing

How Wine Is Made

before the juice begins to pick up the tannins and pigments of the skins and stems. Red wines, on the other hand, are left "on the musts" for a time. The juice is not separated out until some stage of the fermentation process.

FERMENTATION The juice or must is transferred from the press or crusher to a fermentation tank where it is innoculated with a small dose of carefully bred and purified wine yeasts to supplement the yeasts that occur naturally on the grape skins. Fermentation is a process in which the yeasts eat the sugars in the grape juice, turning them into alcohol and carbon dioxide. It takes several hours to get under way, then continues until one of three things happens: all the sugars are consumed, the alcohol content of the new wine kills the yeasts, or alcohol is added to the mixture, killing the yeasts and bringing the process to a halt. As fermentation generates considerable heat, the wine is usually cooled artificially to help keep things under control. For red wines, the juice, or wine, as it now can be called, is pressed from the pomace at some point during or after fermentation. Practice varies with the type of wine.

FIRST RACKING After fermentation, the new wine is transferred to another tank and the lengthy process of clarification is begun. The first stage is called racking. The wine is allowed to stand quietly until most of the material suspended in the wine—dead yeast cells and other by-products of fermentation—settle to the bottom. This residue is known as "the lees." At this point, the almost clear wine is carefully pumped off th

Grape Varieties

top into another set of containers. This first racking is carried out as soon after fermentation as possible and is done quickly to lessen the chance of disagreeable odors being picked up by the wine.

After first racking, most red wines and some whites will go into wooden casks for aging. The wood, usually oak or redwood, imparts some flavor of its own to the wine and allows for a very slow exchange of oxygen and alcohol with the air. During the aging period, other filtering and clarifying or fining processes will be carried out.

Wines that are not aged in wood, such as the lighter whites and most bulk wines, soon undergo final clarification processes. This is followed by other finishing operations: tartrate balancing, ion removal, blending (if any), and bottling. Most wines produced under modern, up-to-date methods are given a final treatment with sulfur dioxide or a microfiltering that makes them sterile before bottling.

Grape Varieties

The taste of a wine is the result of a careful marriage of grape, soil, and climate. It is often the product of centuries of experimentation and selection, but the fruit is the the key. Of the 50 or so varieties of *Vitis vinifera* used in winemaking throughout the world, the 17 listed here are of most concern to a lover of wine.

Barbera—A grape used in the Piedmont region of Italy to make fine, robust red

Grape Varieties

wines, often bearing the name of the grape.

Cabernet Sauvignon—Native to the Bordeaux region of France and the most important component of its great clarets. Cabernet Sauvignon is usually blended with other grapes and is used to make some of the finest red wines of California, Australia, South America, and eastern Europe, as well as Bordeaux. It is a grape of great character and the wines usually require considerable aging.

Chardonnay (Pinot Chardonnay)—The primary white wine grape of Burgundy and Chablis. Chardonnay is also grown with great success in California, producing white wines of great depth and complexity.

Chenin Blanc—A native of France's Loire valley, Chenin Blanc produces white wines ranging from quite dry to flowery and fruity (Vouvray, for example). It has gained great popularity in California where it also makes wines of a surprising range of characters.

Gamay—The grape used to make the ever-popular wines of Beaujolais. It is not particularly successful elsewhere.

Grenache—A native of France's Rhone valley, the Grenache has been exported to most of the important wine producing regions of the world. It is used in the production of rosé wines and in blends of Châteauneuf-du-Pape.

Merlot—One of the secondary grapes of the Bordeaux, used in the blending of the great clarets. In California, Merlot is being used as a varietal as well as being blended with Cabernet Sauvignon.

Nebbiolo—The premiere grape of the Piedmont region of Italy is responsible for Italy's greatest red wines. The wines are long-lasting and slow to mature.

Grape Varieties

Palomino—The grape from which fine sherries are made, both in Spain and California.

Pinot Noir—The great red wine grape of Burgundy. It is used with some success in California and is a component of the great champagnes.

Riesling—The great white wine grape of the Rhine and Moselle valleys—virtually all of Germany's fine wines are Rieslings. The grape is grown with great success in California, Australia, and elsewhere.

Sauvignon Blanc (Fumé Blanc)—Native to Bordeaux, Sauvignon Blanc makes white wines of character ranging from dry and austere to sweet and flowery.

Sémillon—The principal grape of the great dessert wines of Sauternes. It is used to make similar wines in California as well as drier white wines in both areas.

Sylvaner—Makes light, rarely distinguished white wines in Germany, Alsace, California, and elsewhere.

Traminer (Gewürtztraminer)—Makes a spicy, pungent white wine. Grown primarily in Alsace, but also in Germany, Australia, and California.

Trebbiano—The most important white wine grape of central Italy. Used to make Orvieto, Soave, and Chianti.

Zinfandel—A prolific red wine grape of unknown origin that makes wines of surprisingly varied character in the different climates of California's wine country.

Care and Storage

Care and Storage

Wine is a living substance and, like most living things, it responds well to loving care and suffers from maltreatment. The taste that greets your palate when a bottle is opened for drinking depends to a great extent on the care and handling that the wine received on the long journey from vine to table. A wine's positive potential is a product of the vintner's skill, sealed in at bottling time, but its quality can be adversely affected at any later stage. Given reasonable care and proper storage conditions, wines will mature and reach their peak potential at the slow and easy pace that nature intended.

TEMPERATURE People might thrive on change, but wines definitely do not—especially where temperature is concerned. A moderate, constant temperature is the most important single factor in proper wine storage. Rapid, wide, or frequent temperature fluctuations can kill a healthy wine within a few months.

The optimum storage temperature for most wines is about 55°F or 13°C, but temperatures somewhat lower (down to 50°F or 10°C) or higher (up to 75°F or 24°C) are all right as long as they remain constant or change slowly. Cellars are ideal, but confined spaces with exposed heating pipes that heat up and cool off many times a day are deadly for wine storage. Insulating heating pipes in such a situation may make all the difference.

63

Care and Storage

LIGHT Light is another enemy of wine. Its action accelerates oxidation, causing the wine, in effect, to age very rapidly. The stronger the light, the worse the damage. Sunlight is especially destructive. Fortunately, it is seldom a difficult matter to keep one's wine collection out of bright light.

STABILITY A third enemy of wine is vibration or motion. Wines have to be moved occasionally, but the less often the better. Constant vibration has an effect similar to that of temperature change or exposure to light—it causes the wine to become old before its time. For older, heavier red wines, the problem is even more acute. Motion and vibration stir up the sediment, keeping it suspended in the wine rather than allowing it to settle out, thus making the wine undrinkable. So find a spot where your precious bottles can lie quiet and undisturbed.

POSITION Wine bottles are traditionally stored lying flat on their sides with their labels facing up. This allows the wine to be identified without being disturbed. The reason for the recumbent position is to keep the wine in contact with the cork, to prevent its drying out, which would allow air to oxidize and spoil the contents. Most wine racks cradle bottles in the flat position or at a gentle enough slope so that the cork will always be kept moist. Upright storage of wine will lead to trouble.

Few people nowadays have either the space or the money to invest in an extensive wine collection or cellar. Nonetheless, there are some good reasons, both

Care and Storage

practical and economic, to lay down a sizable quantity if you can manage to do so. On the practical side, maintaining a varied and balanced cellar means that wines suitable for all occasions will be on hand when you want them, which should contribute to your overall enjoyment of wine. On the economic side, wines will never be less expensive than when they are first offered for sale. It costs a merchant money to store wine, like anything else, and that added cost is inevitably passed on to you, the buyer. Having ample cellaring space also lets you take advantage of sales, which often offer a case price discount, usually 10 percent off the total cost. The other economic factor operating is rising prices—a combination of inflation and an increasingly tight world market for wines. It's a good bet that wines you buy today will cost substantially more next year, if they are available at all.

SELECTING STORAGE SPACE If you are lucky enough to have an actual cellar, wine storage should be a simple matter. Just select any area away from the furnace, heating pipes, and windows and set up as many racks as you will need. In the absence of a cellar (the situation that most of us face), a cool closet is your next best bet. If your closet is in the interior of the building, that is, not on an outside wall, chances are that the temperature can be kept pretty constant. Closets can be insulated easily, if that should prove necessary. To check the temperature stability of your chosen location, hang a thermometer there and monitor the temperature at frequent intervals for several days.

Vintage Notes

STORAGE RACKS Attractive wine racks of many different kinds are available from wine dealers, department stores, and mail-order houses. While these are satisfactory, most of them are designed to be seen and admired, whereas your wine is better off out of light and out of sight. An easy solution to the storage rack problem is to build simple racks yourself. A diamond-shaped bin, little more than one foot square, will hold an entire case.

FINE TUNING Even in your stable or controlled storage area, some small fluctuations are bound to occur. You can arrange your wines to minimize any adverse effects. Dry white wines are the most perishable and they are best stored near the floor where the changes are least felt. The sturdier red wines are least affected and so will survive perfectly well at the highest levels. In between go the lighter reds and other miscellaneous bottles.

Vintage Notes

The word vintage has taken on a confusing variety of meanings. In its simplest and most direct definition, vintage is the rendering of a given year's grape harvest into wine. The vintage is the birth of each year's new wine and that wine's vintage *date* is the mark of its age.

There are two reasons for putting a vintage date on a wine label. First, it says, "I am important enough that you need to know my age." Wines of high quality are

Vintage Notes

made with the understanding that each will undergo a process of maturing that, depending on the type of wine, is predictable within certain limits. In order to know when a wine is likely to be ready for drinking, its age must be known. Most white and rosé wines and some of the lighter reds will be at their best only for the two or three years after the vintage. Most heavier red wines and a few whites will improve over a period of time—four, five, ten or more years—ultimately reaching a peak of quality which will be maintained for a time, followed by a gradual decline and fading. Knowing the vintage date is essential for keeping track of this history or "taste life."

The second rationale for putting vintage dates on labels is that in certain years, the growing conditions—the complex interacting factors of temperature, sunlight, moisture, wind, and frost—combine in particularly fortunate ways to provide ideal conditions for the grapes to mature, achieving just the right degree of acidity and sweetness, producing wines of good and lasting quality. Of course, there are years in which

67

Bottles & Decanters

the elements conspire in the opposite way, producing poor, undrinkable wines. The caveat here is that designations of "good" and "bad" years are generalizations, even for fairly limited geographical areas—a good or bad year doesn't tell the whole story.

In the first place, so-called microclimates vary greatly within a region. Hail may damage one grower's harvest, leaving that of his neighbor untouched. The difference of a hundred yards may make the difference between a killing frost or none. Then the skill and knowledge of the vintner also come into play. Good winemakers will make better wines than bad or careless ones, in good years and bad. The moral of all this is that while vintage years and vintage charts serve as a general guide, each wine must be judged on its own merits. As one distinguished winemaker has said, "Each year's vintage time requires new answers. No two vintages are the same. But that is what gives wine its charm and beauty."

Bottles & Decanters

You may not be able to tell a book by its cover, but you can certainly identify a wine by its bottle. Like wine glasses, bottles have evolved over time into various shapes traditional to different regions and countries. In a few cases, as with Champagne bottles, the form is functional (the shape and weight of the Champagne bottle enables it to withstand the considerable pressure generated by the gases in the wine), but wine bottle shapes are mostly a means of identification.

Bottles & Decanters

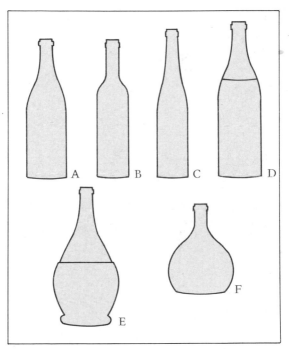

A. The slope-sided bottle is traditional for the wines of Burgundy. Also used where Burgundy's wines are imitated.

B. The Bordeaux bottle has high, rounded shoulders. Used for both red and white wines of that region and in other parts of the world for Cabernet Sauvignons and other Bordeaux-style wines. The same bottle is used to house the finer Chiantis.

C. The tall, slender, gently tapering German bottle. Green for Moselle wines, brown for Rhines.

D. The Champagne bottle.

E. The quaint Chianti flask with its straw basket.

F. This squat bottle, called the *Bocksbeutel*, is used in the Franconia region of Germany. Similar bottles are used for a number of Portuguese and Chilean rosés.

69

Bottles & Decanters

Decanters come in a multitude of sizes and styles. Aside from being clear to allow the beauty of the wine to sparkle through, it doesn't matter what a decanter looks like. Here is a selection.

G. The traditional Italian restaurant or tavern carafe, originally designated to hold a guaranteed quantity of wine, such as a half or full liter. These are popular in American restaurants.

H. The captain's decanter. Its bottom-heavy design prevented it from tipping over in rough seas.

I. Two typical dining table decanters.

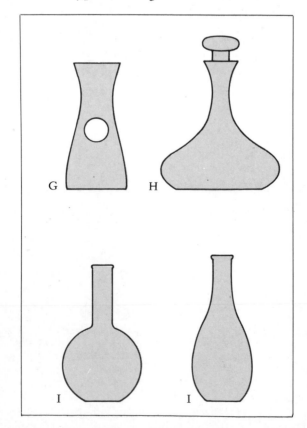

Glasses

Glasses

Fine wines demand fine glasses and pleasing glassware is generally an asset to the enjoyment of any wine. Glasses for table wines need to be simple—roomy, delicate, and clear. Etched, cut, or colored glasses may be fine for martinis, but not for wine.

Various wine-producing regions of the world have evolved their own distinctive styles of glasses over the centuries. Elegant and fanciful shapes are not only designed to please the eye, but, much more important, to enhance the qualities of the wines.
A. The all-purpose wineglass. If you have to make do with a single set of wineglasses —as most of us do—a medium-sized version of the classic French tulip, with a capacity of about nine ounces is fine for just about any table wine you will ever drink. Conventional wisdom states that a glass of red wine may be held in any manner but that white wine whould be held by the stem of the glass so that the wine is not warmed by your hand.
B. This smaller and narrower eight-ounce tulip glass is the preferred vessel for dry white wines.
C. For big, full-bodied reds, the estate-bottled wines of Burgundy and Bordeaux and their equivalents from California and elsewhere, the rounder, more spacious glass known as the Paris goblet is ideal.
D. and E. Champagne and other sparkling wines merit something special. The two traditional champagne glasses are the slender, elongated tulip (D) and the tall, flaring flute (E).

71

Glasses

F. Of the many less known regional specialties, the one most likely to be encountered is the traditional German Rhine wine or hock glass.

G. and **H.** Brandies and cordials require a glass that provides plenty of room for the flavors to vaporize and that then channels the delicious mixture to the nose. The brandy snifter or balloon glass (G) is the familiar choice, while (H) is the shape used in the Cognac region of France.

I. The Spanish *copita*, with its chimney-like shape, is perfect for appreciating the volatile essence of dry sherries and their cousins.

J. and **K.** More familiar bar glasses, the old-fashioned or rock glasses, with or without stem, are excellent for vermouths and similar aperitifs, and for iced drinks generally.

L. The simple tumbler or highball glass, in a variety of sizes is the vessel of choice for tall spritzers and other mixed coolers.

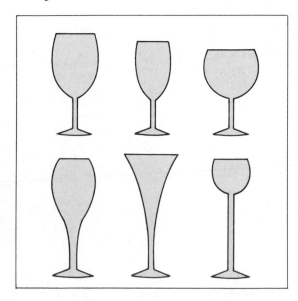

Service

Service

Service

To get the best from your wines, you need to give a little of yourself. While you do not need to become a slave to wine ritual, a modest amount of planning in the serving of wine—getting each wine on the table at the right time and temperature for drinking —will pay big dividends in your pleasure and your guests' enjoyment.

TEMPERATURE The general rule of thumb about temperature is that whites and rosés are drunk chilled, reds are served at room temperature. Like all rules, this fails to take into consideration personal tastes, which always come first. Like many rules, it tends to be followed blindly, with-

Service

out thought. Keep these qualifiers in mind. Most people prefer white and rosé wines on the cool side, but too much chill will kill the flavor of the wine. For reds, room temperature means the temperature of the room where you dine and this may vary greatly from home to home. One man's dining room may be 60°F. and another's 75°F. and therein lies a big difference in drinking.

Sweet dessert wines—the Sauternes, Barsacs, Champagnes, and their equivalents—are generally served the coldest, usually around 40°F. (5°C.). Dry, young whites and rosés are generally drunk at temperatures of 45 to 50°F. (7 to 10°C.). Some mature whites come into their own at a slightly warmer temperature, around 55°F. (13°C.).

Young, light red wines, like Beaujolais, are often drunk at a cool temperature in the 60°F. (16°C.) range. This is, by the way, moderate cellar temperature.

The bigger, older red wines are drunk at the warmest—around 65°F. (18°C.) or slightly warmer.

Again, it should be made clear that these are *average* or *typical* figures. If you *like* white wines at 75°F., that is the temperature at which you should drink them.

COOLING   The quickest way to cool wine is in an ice bucket or wine cooler containing one-third water and two-thirds crushed ice with enough room left over for the bottle. About 20 minutes in the ice bucket will cool a bottle to about 45°; 30 minutes lowers the temperature to 40°. The refrigerator is slower—it takes between 1½ and 2½ hours to achieve the same degree of cooling.

Service

BREATHING Virtually all still wines benefit from a period of exposure to the air before they are drunk. This breathing period gives the wine's flavors a chance to wake up. Whites and rosés generally require only a short time—15 minutes or so—to come alive. Reds take longer, and the younger the wine, the longer the breathing, or aeration time required to bring them to their best. A young, vigorous red wine full of tannin may benefit from three or four hours of breathing time. The more mature the wine, the less time is required. Past a certain point in time, say 20 to 30 years, aeration becomes unnecessary, and in fact, a race begins to drink the wine before its ephemeral flavors evanesce.

UNCORKING To drink a wine it is necessary to uncork it first, whatever else you may say. The object here is to get the bottle open without getting cork into the wine and shaking up the bottle.

Cut off the lead capsule that covers the cork and neck of the bottle. The usual method is to cut cleanly around the lip with a knife, leaving the remainder on the neck, but removing the capsule entirely is perfectly all right. Next comes the drawing of the cork proper.

Of the staggering number of corkscrews available today, one of the simplest and perhaps the best is the tool of professionals and *sommeliers*, often dubbed the waiter's friend. It consists of an open spiral screw, which grips the cork more securely than any other type, mounted in the center of a bar that has a sturdy knife blade hinged on one end and a special lever, notched to engage the lip of the bottle, hinged on the other. The knife is perfect for cutting the   75 foil capsule along with any wires that might be present.

To draw the cork, drive the screw carefully into the center of the cork with a twisting motion. Ideally, it should penetrate the entire length of the cork *without* emerging at the bottom; this is to avoid getting fragments of cork into the wine. The lever is then propped on the lip of the bottle, and the cork is easily removed by lifting the opposite end of the bar. Do be careful to avoid shaking the bottle during this operation. Give the neck of the bottle a careful wipe with a towel, inside and out, before the wine is served.

DECANTING   There are three reasons for decanting wine. First, wine is beautiful to look at and cannot be seen to advantage in its green or brown bottle. Second, decanting accomplishes the breathing or aeration process better and more quickly than simply letting the bottle stand open. Third, in the case of mature red wines that contain sediments, the sound wine must be poured off from the dregs in order to be enjoyed without fear of contamination. There is nothing toxic about wine sediment, it just ruins the taste of the wine.

In keeping with the first of these reasons, decanters should be of clear glass so that the color of the wine will show true, in all its glory.

The decanting of a mature red wine should begin a day or two ahead of time, if done by the book. The bottle should be brought from the cellar and stood upright in a cool, quiet spot so that the sediment will settle to the bottom. (Don't worry, the cork will not dry out in this short time.) Several hours before serving, the wine should be uncorked *carefully*, so as not to disturb the sediment. The decanter should be clean and dry. The pouring from the bottle into the decanter is traditionally done with a candle or other light under the neck of the bottle so the wine and the dregs can be clearly seen. The wine is poured slowly and steadily into the decanter, stopping immediately when the first sediment nears the neck of the bottle. Far better to waste half a glass than to ruin the entire bottle. That's all there is to it. Younger reds and whites are even simpler—just open the bottle, wipe the neck, and transfer the contents into the decanter.

Aperitifs

Aperitifs are designed to gently stimulate the appetite and tastebuds. They are meant to relax the spirit rather than gratify the desire for a slug of grain-distilled alcohol that might diminish the tensions of the day.

SHERRY History's premier aperitif is sherry. The name of this pale gold or amber-hued fortified wine comes from an anglicized pronunciation of the town of Jerez de la Frontera, one of the three important towns in southern Spain's sherry region.

Although the only true sherry is created primarily from Palomino grapes in the province of Cadiz, through the years, wines labeled sherry have been produced in many countries besides Spain, most notably in the United States and Australia. To understand sherry, is is necessary to view it as a Spanish wine. The first fermentation of

77

Aperitifs

Spanish sherry requires approximately three months after the harvest. During this period, as the sugar ferments into alcohol, air circulates in the oak casks. When the fermentation is complete, the wine is sampled and an evaluation is made by the vintners. They check to determine the degree to which the wine has attained a thick coating of yeast cells called *flor* (Spanish for flower) on its surface. This is the moment when the wines, as the Spaniards say, "declare themselves."

The wine that declares itself a *fino* has a thick coating of *flor*. The alcoholic content will eventually reach 15 to 16 percent. To encourage the development of *flor*, the casks are not quite filled to the top and are loosely stoppered so that oxygen circulates freely.

If a thin coating of surface *flor* is present, the wine is an *amontillado*.

Oloroso sherry has no *flor* at all. When this is discovered, the wine is fortified with up to 18 percent brandy to prevent development of *flor*.

Each type—fino, amontillado, and oloroso—matures for up to three years before being integrated into the *solera* system.

In the solera system, the reclassified sherry is poured into casks. As sherry is drawn off from the older casks at the bottom, the newer sherry moves down through the system. The process takes about 20 years—adding richness to the olorosos and keeping the finos fresh.

Only one-third of the oldest sherry may be removed from the solera in any given year. Before bottling, the sherry is clarified using egg whites beaten with a whisk made of thyme branches. When the mixture is added to the wine, it sinks to the bottom

Aperitifs

Fino

JEREZ XÉRÈS SHERRY

CONSEJO REGULADOR
DE LA DENOMINACIÓN DE ORIGEN

A Spanish sherry label

Information may include:

Type of sherry: Fino, Amontillado, Manzanilla, Oloroso, or Cream.
Name of shipper and importer.
Guarantee that sherry is from Spain.

of the cask, absorbing all the suspended sediment. When the wine is drawn off, it is clear and is said to have "fallen bright."

In addition to the clarification process, the sherry is refrigerated for several days

before bottling. This insures that the wine will be bright in the bottle, even if exposed to very low temperatures.

Another fortification with brandy is made just before bottling. The final alcoholic content of sherry ranges from 17 to 22 percent.

The sherry styles are as follows:

Fino — light and dry.

Manzanilla — the lightest and finest fino produced in *bodegas* of Sanlucar de Barrameda, a town located at the apex of the sherry triangle. There is a wonderful sea breeze that adds a special quality to the sherry.

Amontillado — has a slightly higher alcoholic content than the average fino and is darker in color. Signs of an amontillado being born are an increasing nutty taste and a darkening of the *flor*.

Oloroso — dry, dark full-bodied sherries. They have an opalescent quality.

Cream — a blend of dry oloroso with a distillation from the Pedro Ximénez grape.

Although these are general classifications, each bodega makes its sherry slightly differently, so the range of sweet to dry in each category may be considerable.

Sherry should be stored in a cool, dark place but need not be racked. The lighter sherries should be drunk within six months of bottling. Heavier, sweeter types will last longer.

Although the Sherry region in Spain is the only one allowed to use the name without a qualifier of location, many other countries produce sherry-type wines: Jura in France, Germany, South Africa, Cyprus, and the United States, where California vintners have made sherry an important part of their stock. Outside Spain, the *flor*

Aperitifs

is not naturally achieved, so the yeast is cultured and injected into the wine.

MONTILLA Just a bit more than a stone's throw from the famous sherry district lies Montilla-Moriles where the Pedro Ximénez grape grows in the chalky soil virtually identical to that of the sherry triangle. But because Montilla didn't have the same political clout, it has been relegated to a separate and unequal position. Its wines cannot be classified without the addition of the Montilla name. The sherry-types of Montilla have a substantially higher sugar content and therefore do not often have to be fortified. The alcoholic content reaches 16 to 20 percent without the addition of the brandy.

MADEIRA The island of Madeira lies off the coast of North Africa. Colonized by the Portuguese, the island has been producing a blended wine called Madeira for over 400 years.

In the old days, the wine-filled casks were used as ballast in ships. It was discovered that the heat and agitation in the hold improved the wine immeasurably. Today the grape juice is fermented for almost a month, producing *vinho claro* or clear wine. Fortifying Maderia brandy is added and the casks are moved to a room where the temperature is kept at 130°F. After cooking for three to six months, more brandy is added (depending on the wine's classification) and as *vinho generoso*, it is allowed to mature before being shipped. There are two aperitif Madeiras: Sercial, which is light but more full-bodied than a sherry fino, and Verdelho, which is sweeter than Sercial and tastes of honey and smoke. Rainwater,

81

Aperitifs

a generic term, is much in demand for cooking. Bual and Malmsey are dessert wines.

VERMOUTH   The base of vermouth is white wine and each vermouth manufacturer has a secret recipe for adding such essences as wormwood, juniper, orange peel, coriander, quinine, and other exotic things.

The process involves the infusion of the herb essences into an alcohol base. Sometimes the mixture is heated to increase the flavor. Then it is added to a mixture of the white wine that has been combined with _mistelle_ (unfermented grape juice and brandy) or sugar syrup. Blending takes place in huge vats. Wooden paddles are used to keep irrelevant tastes out of the blend, clarifier is added, then the mixture is pasteurized and refrigerated for a couple of weeks. Before it is bottled, the vermouth is filtered again to remove any precipitants.

Vermouth may be red or white, sweet or dry. Cinzano, Martini, and Gaucia produce both kinds. Noilly Pratt is dry only. Chambéry is a light, dry French vermouth made by a slightly different process.

WINE-BASED APERITIFS   Dubonnet is probably the best known. Created in France, it is now produced in the United States and in France. It is a sweetened red or white vermouth incorporating bitter bark and quinine. The recipes for both versions are trade secrets. The white Dubonnet is somewhat drier.

Byrrh (pronounced beer) is red wine fortified with brandy and flavored with quinine.

St.-Raphaël has the same ingredients as

Byrrh but in different proportions.

Lillet is a blend of brandy and sweetened red or white wine.

Champagne

Since the early eighteenth century experiments of a monk named Dom Perignon, virtually all champagnes have been blends. Most superior champagnes are blends of grapes from four large districts in the French environs of Reims and Epernay.

Those grapes are dominated by the Pinot Noir (the red wine grape of Burgundy), Pinot Meunier, Chardonnay, and Pinot Blanc. The Pinot Noir, whose juice is white and will stay that way if removed quickly enough from the grape skins, gives this blended wine a wonderful strength and vitality. The Chardonnay and Pinot Blanc bring delicacy.

The unique process of making champagne begins with the harvesting of the grapes, set by official decree about 100 days after the first flowering of the vines. Grapes are sold to producers before they are picked and are priced according to earlier ratings. The actual harvesting takes about 12 days.

Once the grapes are taken to the press, time is of the essence. To avoid contaminating the wine with the grape skins, special large presses are used which allow the juice to percolate quickly. Champagne made from the juice of the first pressing is called "vin de cuvée." Second and third pressings are used for still champagne wine marketed as "vin nature de la champagne."

Each four-ton pressing results in 2,666

Champagne

liters of juice which is divided into 13 "pieces." The first 10 pieces comprise the *cuvee*, the basic grape juice of champagne and is superior to the other pressings.

Large oak or cement casks are used to store the wine during the cleansing process when sediment and foreign bodies are removed. The juice is then drawn off into 205-litre barrels, carefully labeled with the source of the contents, and transported to the chalk cellars of the major champagne producers.

First fermentation takes about three weeks. The wine is racked off under cooler temperatures, which helps precipitate any sediment so that it can be removed. The *cuvée* is an individual house blend made from the various *crus* or growths from specific vineyards. The *chef de cave* (or cellarmaster) mixes similar *crus*, then adds different proportions of many others to create the *coupage*. Classic champagne is made from a blend of Pinot Noir and Chardonnay, but there is a trend toward the Blanc de Blanc type which is exclusively Chardonnay.

Reserve wine from older, great vintages is added for depth. True vintage champagne is rare but sometimes available when there has been a particularly outstanding year.

The second fermentation of the wine adds the sparkle to champagne. The *cuvee* is put into tanks, then natural fermenting agents, sugar, and wine are added. When bottled, the sugar in the wine is converted to alcohol and carbon dioxide gas—the gas is contained and bubbles are formed.

The wine ferments in the cool chalk cellars for as long as four years. The wine begins forming sediment, so the bottles are moved to sloping racks where a man rotates them periodically to move the sediment

Champagne

closer to the cork. This method is called *remuage*. The whole operation takes about three months.

Then the bottles are stacked vertically, with the neck down, and are run through a freezing brine solution. This further consolidates the sediment and in the wonderful pop of *dégorgement*, the sediment is removed along with a bit of the sparkling wine.

Champagne is checked again at this point for perfect transparency. The bottle is topped off with more wine of the same *cuvée* and a little more sugar solution called *dosage*. The proportion of sugar added depends on how dry the cellarmaster wants to make the champagne. It ranges from *brut*, the driest, to *sec, demi-sec,* and *doux*, the sweetest.

In addition to the differences between dry and sweet champagne, various champagne houses blend their wines in three general categories:

Light: Taittinger, Ayala, Laurent-Perrier, Charbaut & Fils, Charles Heidsieck, Henriot, Jacquesson, and any Blanc de Blancs.

Medium: Piper-Heidsieck, Pommery, Canard-Duchêne, Moët et Chandon, Ruinart Père & Fils, Perrier-Jouet, G. H. Mumm, and De Venoge.

Full: Bollinger, Krug, Pol Roger, Lanson, Louis Roederer, and Veuve Clicquot-Ponsardin.

Sparkling wine produced in the Champagne region is the only type that can be called French Champagne. However if the process used is the one described earlier, known as *méthode champenoise*, the name champagne may be used on the label with an additional location appellation, as in Domaine Chandon Napa Valley Brut Champagne.

Champagne

There are several spectacular California champagnes. At least two wineries, Schramsberg and Domain Chandon, make only champagne. Chandon, as the name implies, was founded by the Moët firm which produced its first bottles in 1976. Most California wineries use the same type of grapes as do the French, and depending on the dosage, the champagne is rated as follows: natural, very rare and without any dosage added; brut; extra dry; dry or *sec*; and sweet or *doux*. Leading firms are Almaden Korbel, Hanns Kornell, Masson, Beaulieu, and Weibel.

New York State vintners who use the *méthode champenoise* are Gold Seal, Great Western, Taylor, and Widmer. California wine is blended with the locally grown Catawba and Delaware grapes which produces a sweet champagne that is labeled extra dry. The driest type is known as brut special.

There are several methods and many other countries that make excellent sparkling wines.

The tank method ferments the wine a second time in a tank, where the dosage is added.

The impregnation method injects carbon dioxide gas into white wine with a high alcoholic content.

Sekt is a German sparkling wine and because the dosage added is so high in sugar, the quality of the grapes used in blending does not have to be very good. They use the tank method.

In Portugal, sparkling wine is known as Espumante. The best are Raposeira and Messias which are both brut, as well as Borges Royal Brut.

The Spanish Xampáns or Gran Cremants

are sparkling and the extra bruts of Castell-blanch and Cordoniu made by the *méthode champenoise* are recommended.

The most famous sparking wine of Italy is Asti Spumante. Another sweet spumante widely available is called Lacrima Christi ("Tears of Christ").

In Argentina, all three major methods of producing sparkling wine are used. Moët et Chandon has recently established a winery there, blending Chardonnay, Ugni Blanc, and Sémillon grapes.

Argentina

For years the people of Argentina consumed their own product in such quantities that virtually none was left over for export. Recently, as interest in Argentinian wine has grown tremendously due to the rising costs of similar European wines, production has expanded to answer the demand. The rest of the world is now getting an opportunity to enjoy these excellent wines.

A little more than a century ago Italian immigrants revolutionized Argentinian wine-producing techniques and established an essential irrigation system that brings snow water from the Andes into the formerly barren Mendoza plain. Wine making is the only important industry in the state of Mendoza, contributing 70 percent of Argentina's production and half of the wine production of the South American continent. There are more than 40,000 growers, but 20 percent of all production is controlled by nine firms.

Traditionally, the Criolla grape has dominated wine production, but now the Mal-

87

Australia

bec is drawing close, followed by Cabernet and Pinot Noir. Most wine experts agree that the Cabernet Sauvignon is the best wine of Argentina.

Generally, the reds are considered superior to the whites. But there is increasing promise for the Rieslings and Pinot Blancs of the Rio Negro area south of Mendoza. These vineyards account for nearly 5 percent of the country's production.

Australia

Australian still wines are relative newcomers to most tables because a combination of import duties and local consumption kept most of these excellent wines out of the export market. Recently, some Australian wine has been finding its way into the world market—and it has been welcomed.

Australia's history of wine making dates from the days of the first permanent settlers over 150 years ago when French and German vine stocks were brought to the Hunter River Valley area of New South Wales. Today, the Hunter River Valley wineries, family-owned for generations, produce table wines. With the Chardonnay grape and a new process of fermenting white grapes in sealed vats at a cold temperature, the wines are light and dry.

Two of the largest and best-known vintners are Lindeman and Penfold. McWilliams also is known for good white wine that is produced in Hanwood.

In Victoria, the Great Western area produces fine red and white wines. The Chateau Tahbilk bottle holds an exceptional

red that needs quite a few years of aging, but eventually develops a wonderful, complex bouquet.

Sixty-five percent of the country's wine is produced in South Australia. Germans, with memories of the Rhineland grapes, were the primary settlers of the area's Barossa Valley, and many feel that the area's best wine is the Rhine Riesling which is shipped by Yalumba and Gramps, among others. The Barossa Valley co-op markets wine under the name of Kaiserstuhl.

Because the major vintners in South Australia own property throughout the country, grapes are often blended. For instance, Seppelt's blends the grapes from Victoria in Western Australia, resulting in a distinctive red wine.

The oldest vineyard in the Southern Vales is Reynella. Other names to look for are Seaview and Tintara.

Coonawara, the southernmost Australian vineyard, produces Australia's best red wines, in many experts' opinions.

Canada

Although one doesn't normally think of Canada as a wine-producing and -exporting nation, the quality and growing quantity of these wines are making a significant impact in the world market.

Canada possesses two important vine-growing regions: the Niagara Peninsula in the province of Ontario, responsible for three-quarters of the wine produced in the province; and the Okanagan Valley in the province of British Columbia, which pro-

duces about 10 percent of the nation's wine.

These areas have mild winters because the harsh climate is moderated by the proximity to large bodies of water. Curiously enough, if you check the latitude (43rd to 50th parallels), the Canadian wine regions are within the same boundaries as some of the greatest vineyards of Europe.

Canada's early explorers found grapes growing wild and made wine from them. Originally, they included varieties of the Labrusca grape that now have been developed into the following types: Concord for red wine; Catawba for pink; and Elvira and Niagara for white. All of these vines produce a sweet wine and all of them have a hint of what wine experts call "foxiness" which means it has a strong, pungent bouquet. But Canada's taste for wine has changed to a preference for drier wines—thus hybrid grapes have been developed, particularly in Ontario.

Today, the leading white wine grapes are: the Aurora, a soft medium-dry; Dutchess, a crisp, spicy taste; Pinot Chardonnay, firm and dry; and Seyval Blanc, a soft, semi-dry grape. The major red wine grapes are: Chelois, a full-bodied dry wine; de Chaunac, a medium- to light-bodied, fruity wine named after an oenologist who developed many hybrids in Canada; Gamay, medium-to light-bodied red wines and a medium-dry white wine; Maréchal Foch, a hybrid developed from the Pinot Noir that makes a medium- to full-bodied red wine.

Wine production began later in British Columbia than in Ontario. Around the turn of the twentieth century, the local wineries brought grapes up from California and then produced the wine under their own labels. Today, however, they grow

Canada

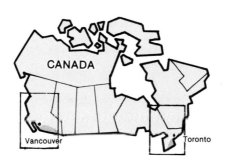

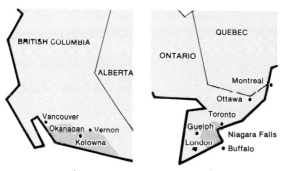

their own grapes and vinify them locally.

Technology contributes additional sophistication to Canadian wines. The use of refrigeration controls the speed of fermentation; thus, a more delicate, drier wine can be coaxed along. Canadians do a lot of blending but, in Ontario, by regulation, a varietal wine must have at least 75 percent of a single variety for it to appear on the label. Vintage wine must contain 85 percent of the wine produced of that year.

The Ontario Grape and Wine Standards Committee, which is made up of government and growers' representatives, can declare a wine to be Ontario Superior, once it has met their basic standards and has been taste-tested for better quality. The Government Liquor Board, which distributes most Canadian wine, also requires a listing of sugar content on the wine label.

California

California

The winelands of California are, for the most part, located within a 100-mile radius of San Francisco. The earliest wineries were located near Sonoma and the Napa valley to the north. These areas, particularly the Napa valley, continued to be the most important producing regions until recently, when the need for expansion forced growers to seek out new territory. Although there had been a number of vineyards south of San Francisco in Santa Clara and Monterey counties, vineyard acreage has expanded dramatically in that region over the past ten years. Excellent wines are being produced in places where no grapes grew 15 years ago. As demand for wine makes the business more profitable, new climate niches suitable for fine wine grapes will continue to open up all over the state.

The California wine industry is, and always has been, more than the fine wine trade. California started as a producer of large quantities of wine at reasonable prices, and still does this successfully. But the serious small producers have raised the quality of the bulk producers by educating the public palate and creating demand for a better product. The bulk wines are substantially higher in quality than their French or Italian counterparts—the carafe wines or *vins du pays* consumed on an everyday basis by people for whom wine drinking is a centuries-old tradition—no mean achievement for an industry that is, comparatively speaking, in its infancy. California produces

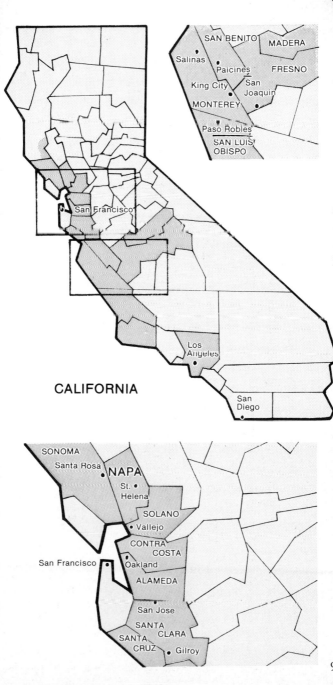

California

SAN BENITO
MADERA
Salinas
Paicines
FRESNO
King City
San
Joaquin
MONTEREY
Paso Robles
SAN LUIS
OBISPO

San Francisco

Los
Angeles

CALIFORNIA

San
Diego

SONOMA
Santa Rosa
NAPA
St.
Helena
SOLANO
Vallejo
CONTRA
COSTA
San Francisco
Oakland
ALAMEDA
San Jose
SANTA
CLARA
SANTA
CRUZ
Gilroy

93

California

hundreds of millions of gallons of bulk wines yearly, made mostly from grapes grown in the warm, fertile San Joaquin valley to the west of the fine wine country.

Visitors to wine country should take advantage of the area's many vineyard tours. Vintner members of the California Wine Institute (virtually all California wine growers) who offer tours of their wineries are listed in a book, *California Wine Wonderland*, published by the Institute. Many of the tours can be accomplished during a day trip from San Francisco or Los Angeles.

You can get a copy of this excellent directory listing visiting days and times for all participating wineries by sending a request and a self-addressed envelope to the California Wine Institute, 165 Post Street, San Francisco, California 94108.

Most wineries are open to visitors throughout the year. The fall harvest is perhaps the most active wine-making period and is the most crowded time for visitors. To maximize your enjoyment and avoid crowds try to visit during the week. But as Robert Lawrence Balzer states in his book *Wines of California*, "In a word, the best time for you to come to the vineyard is when you have the most time to spend."

Most of the better wines now being made in California are made from European grape stocks. Both logic and standard California practice suggest dealing with wines as varietals.

The big two in California are French grapes: Cabernet Sauvignon, the great red wine grape of Bordeaux, and Pinot Chardonnay, the great white wine grape of Burgundy. Cabernet Sauvignon is probably the most successful and highest-quality grape grown in California.

California

The California grape retains the same varietal taste it has in Bordeaux, and makes big, velvety, fruity wines of great power. Cabernets are built to mature more quickly in California than in France, so they are bolder and perhaps less elegant. In blind tastings over recent years, however, much to the horror of the French, California Cabernets have consistently been ranked with the top French growths.

The Chardonnay grape has also been immensely successful in California. Like the Cabernet Sauvignon, it is a slow-maturing and low-yielding grape, so the wines are expensive to produce. Many apparently feel that the results more than justify the effort and expense. While no one is yet comparing California Chardonnays to Montrachet, the time for that comparison may not be far off.

The Merlot grape, grown in Bordeaux for blending with the Cabernet Sauvignon, is grown and produced as a separate varietal wine, quite heavy in character. Production of varietal Merlots is still in its infancy.

Pinot Noir, the great red wine grape of Burgundy, is grown extensively in California but not quite as successfully as Cabernet Sauvignon. The characteristic taste of the grape doesn't develop in the same way in California. But as new wine growing territories are opened up, the hope of finding the perfect niche for Pinot Noir remains.

Chenin Blanc, the grape from which the lucious wines of Vouvray are made, does splendidly in California. It responds to different micro-climates by yielding wines of widely varying character. Recent Chenin Blancs have ranged from quite dry to rather sweet, but always with a very spicy, fruity taste.

Another white wine grape that has proved successful in California is the Riesling. The true German grape is referred to in California as White or Johannisberg Riesling to distinguish it from other, lesser grapes bearing the same name. No particular attempt has been made to mimic the taste of German wines; this is one instance in which the product of the marriage of New World soil and Old World grape has been allowed to speak for itself. The wines are crisp and aromatic.

Both the Sauvignon Blanc and Sémillon grape, the two components of the great wines of Sauternes, are grown in California. The former is used primarily to make rather dry, aromatic wines, often called Fumé Blanc (white smoke or smoked white).

California

The latter produces wines that tend toward sweetness and a dessert-wine quality. Some wine makers in California are experimenting with the Botrytis mold that produces the famous dessert wines of Sauternes. It is early in that game and results have been mixed so far.

Two grapes called Gamay are grown in California. Confusingly, the one commonly referred to as Gamay Beaujolais is not related to the French Gamay at all. The grape called Napa Gamay *is* the grape of southern Burgundy. Both make light, summertime reds, neither bearing much resemblance to the wine of Beaujolais.

The Petite Sirah is another grape that arouses some confusion and controversy in California. It is generally believed to be the grape that makes the great red wines of the Rhône valley, but there is some doubt. Many experts say that there is some genuine French Syrah in California, but most of the grapes bearing that name are an inferior variety of Pinot Noir. If true, that would explain why so little fine wine has been produced under the name Petite Sirah. Another explanation is that the matching of grape to climate necessary for the best results is only now beginning to succeed for the Petite Sirah. This conclusion is supported by recent production of some new areas. The best Petite Sirahs are dark, rich, strong-flavored wines.

Zinfandel, a grape whose origin is somewhat a mystery—many experts consider it to be an indigenous species—has proven to be an astonishingly adaptable variety. It grows in a broad range of climatic conditions and makes wines of widely ranging character—from light, young, and fruity to rather elegant, soft, and well-aging. The grape has a characteristic varietal taste that comes through in all the wines.

In keeping with the tendency of California producers to make many, many different wines—to offer an entry to fill every slot in the marketplace—many wineries began producing sparkling wines that are known as champagnes. Champagne making has now become a serious business in California. Several makers have begun specializing in champagnes over the last two decades, and their products have reflected the attention devoted to their making. At least one venerable French champagne producer has bought acreage in California and is going into production in direct competition with the native product.

In the absence of a centuries-old tradition, the nomenclature of California wines has been somewhat confused and a subject of much controversy. During the early days, most of the wine was produced in bulk. It was blended from many grapes in an attempt to satisfy a theoretical typical taste. In an endeavor to make their product attractive, producers and marketers attached names of well-known French wines—most typically Chablis, Sauterne, and Burgundy—to the jugs they sold. While this might have made the product more interesting to the American buying public, it told the buyer nothing about the wine and aroused the resentment of both the French, whose noble names were being pirated, and those serious wine drinkers who appreciated what California was capable of and felt that the wines should be what they were, rather than aping the French.

As fine California wines gained more acceptance and more growers began producing them, another system of nomen-

Chile

clature was established—wines are now identified by the grape varieties from which they are made. While this system answered many criticisms, it did not lay all controversy to rest. The varietal designation requires that the wine bearing the name contain at least 51 percent of the grape whose name it bears. This means that heavily blended wines can be sold under the same name as wines made from 100 percent of the same grape. There has been as yet no legislated solution to this problem, although there is an active movement to raise the varietal requirement to 75 percent. Under the current honor system, growers and winemakers with reputations for excellence make the finest possible wine from each variety and price them accordingly. Another movement currently gaining some acceptance among the serious wine producers is the inclusion of place names along with the varietal name and sometimes adding the name of a particular favored vineyard.

Chile

The Chilean government, which encourages the development of cooperative vineyards through federal loans, is progressive in its nurturing of the wine industry. Most of the private holdings are of only a few acres and cultivation methods vary widely.

There are strict governmental controls. Each resident is allowed a yearly consumption of 60 liters. Any production beyond the quotas is used for export or for distillation of industrial alcohol. Additionally, the National Council of External Commerce regulates the alcohol content, clarity, and age of export wine. The following designations appear: *courant*, wine aged one year which is the minimum for export; *special*, aged two years; *reserve*, aged three years; and *gran vino*, aged six years.

Although wine production was initiated by the Jesuit missionaries, the father of Chilean wine was Silvestre Ochagavia who imported French vines to the country's middle region in 1851.

Today the Maipo River valley is considered an outstanding location for table wine production, although the Aconcaqua valley is not far behind. The top bodegas (vintners) are located in the environs of the capital city, Santiago. They include Vina Cusino at Macul, Underraga, Concha y Toro, and Santa Rita in the Maipo valley. The vineyard at Cusino Macul has vines from original cuttings imported from Pauillac and Martillac in Graves.

France

There is general agreement among wine lovers that of all the world's wine-producing nations, France reigns supreme. France does not produce the most wine, but it does produce the largest number of significant wine types, and, above all, it produces the wines that vintners throughout the world consider as the standard of quality.

One of the unique contributions made by the French to the practice of winemaking was the legal system developed over the first quarter of this century resulting in the

France

well-known *Appellation Contrôlée*. It was an attempt by the government to deal with the chaotic, pathetic condition of the once noble wine trade in a country that had been devastated by the phylloxera plague and corruption.

In simplest terms, the law requires that wines bearing labels with an *Appellation Contrôlée* (the officially sanctioned place-name of origin) are grown and produced within the area designated and that they are made from the grapes traditionally used in the making of the wines of the area. The degree of specificity varies with the region. There is a parallel system dealing with the wines of lesser districts known as *Vins Délimités de Qualité Supérieure* (abbreviated V.D.Q.S.). The government, in effect, vouches for the quality of the product. The result of all this regulation is that very high standards are met by wine growers and vintners in all the major producing areas of France. The way the appellation works is that it is exclusive. Bordeaux is one appellation, and it covers a great deal of territory. Within Bordeaux are several smaller appellations, one of which is the Médoc. Within the Médoc are four towns or communes each with its own appellation. The more specific the appellation, the smaller the area delineated by the name and the higher the indication of quality. A wine from Château Margaux, for example, has the right to call itself *Appellation Bordeaux Contrôlée*, but the *Appellation Margaux Contrôlée* is a much higher indication of quality.

The *Appellation Contrôlée* system contributes to the simplicity and constancy of French labeling practices. A French wine label usually begins with the name of the place the wine was made, be it château, 101

France

vineyard, commune, cooperative, or district, followed by the most specific *Appellation Contrôlée* to which the wine is entitled, the vintage of the wine, and the proprietor's or vintner's name and address. There might be some designation such as *Grand Cru* (great growth), or *Cru Exceptionelle* (exceptional growth), or some other rating earned by the wine in the first systematic classification of the fine wines of France in 1855. A statement such as *Mis en Bouteilles au Château* or *Mis en Bouteilles au Domaine*, indicates the wine was bottled at the place where it was made. The former is an indication of quality, the latter a guarantee of authenticity.

The Bordeaux district is perhaps the most important wine-producing region in the world—in terms of quantity of high quality. The city of Bordeaux is certainly the world's most important wine city. The District contains a number of sub-regions— the most important are Pomerol, St. Émilion, Graves, Sauternes, Barsac, and the Médoc, the largest and most important. The fine wines of Pomerol and St. Émilion are big, fragrant reds. Graves produces a large quantity of dry white wines often described as thin. The remaining region, the Médoc, is responsible for most of the truly exceptional red wines of Bordeaux. The red wines of the district are made primarily from the Cabernet Sauvignon grape, but it is always blended with one or more lesser grapes for balance and finish.

Burgundy is no less important than Bordeaux in the greatness of its finest products, but it is more difficult to define geographically and lags far behind in the quantity of its fine wines. The true Burgundy wine district is the strip known as the Côte d'Or

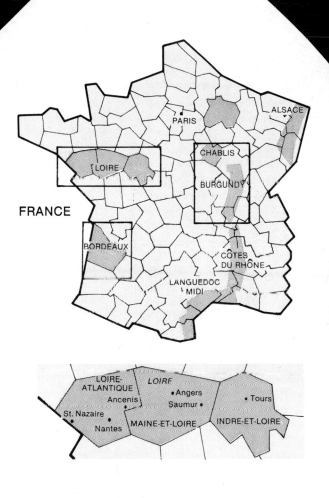

France

FRANCE

PARIS

ALSACE

CHABLIS

LOIRE

BURGUNDY

BORDEAUX

CÔTES
DU RHÔNE

LANGUEDOC
MIDI

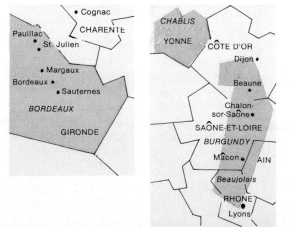

LOIRE-
ATLANTIQUE

LOIRE

Angers

Ancenis

Saumur

Tours

St. Nazaire

MAINE-ET-LOIRE

INDRE-ET-LOIRE

Nantes

Cognac

CHARENTE

Pauillac

St. Julien

Margaux

Bordeaux

Sauternes

BORDEAUX

GIRONDE

CHABLIS

YONNE

CÔTE D'OR

Dijon

Beaune

Chalon-
sor-Saône

SAÔNE-ET-LOIRE

BURGUNDY

Mâcon

AIN

Beaujolais

RHONE

Lyons

(the Gold Coast), but other sub-regions to the north and south have become identified the Burgundy and are considered part of it. To the north is the tiny, but significant, district of Chablis. Like the other white wines of Burgundy, Chablis wines are made exclusively from the noble Pinot Chardonnay, a slow-maturing, slight-yielding grape. The wines are acidic, fruity, and tend to have a flinty or chalky taste, from the chalky soil of the countryside.

The Côte d'Or is divided into two regions, the Côte de Nuits and the Côte de Beaune, each named for its principal town. The significant wines of the Côte de Nuits are nearly all reds and include most of the truly great Burgundies. All the reds of the Côte d'Or are made from the Pinot Noir grape which produces a smooth, velvety wine with a good fruity taste and a slight sparkle. The warmer climate of the Côte de Beaune produces a mixture of red and white wines. The reds of this region are lighter and less long-lived than those made to the north. The whites, however, are the greatest still white wines made in France—big, deep, and complex. The greatest white wine vineyard in Burgundy is Montrachet and many surrounding towns have attached their names to it. This common practice in Burgundy makes for some rather confusing nomenclature.

Further to the south, more or less centered around the towns of Chalon, Mâcon and Lyon, are the regions known as the Chalonnais, Mâconnais and Beaujolais. Pouilly-Fuissé, another hearty product of the Chardonnay grape, is the most notable wine of the Chalonnais. Mâcon produces both good whites from Chardonnay and sound red wines made from a combination

France

of Pinot Noir and Gamay. Finally, Beaujolais, the warm southern extreme of greater Burgundy, produces the immensely popular light red wines made from the Gamay grape that are drunk before their second birthdays.

Continuing southward along the Rhône valley the wine traveler encounters first the Côte Rotie (the roasted slope) and Hermitage. These regions produce big, hearty, long-lasting red wines from the Syrah grape. These wines spend several years in the cask and might require as many as 20 or 30 years in the bottle to reach their peak.

At Avignon, down river from Hermitage, lies the district with the intriguing name of Châteauneuf-du-Pape (the new château of the Pope), so named for the time when the papal seat was at Avignon. The primary grape of this area is the Grenache, which makes the full-bodied red that takes the district name of Châteauneuf-du-Pape. Across the river in Tavel the Grenache is made into a rosé, one of the few such wines to receive any recognition in or out of France.

The Loire valley is covered with vines along most of its 600-mile length. The notable wines, starting to the east of the Loire headwaters, include Pouilly-Fumé and Sancerre, two dry, flinty whites. Further west are the vineyards of Vouvray. Planted with the Chenin Blanc grape that has found favor recently in California, Vouvray produces white wines, both dry and sweet. The latter have unusual aromatic floweriness and sometimes show a slight effervescence. Toward the mouth of the Loire, near the city of Nantes, a light, dry, flowery white wine known as Muscadet is produced. The area has only recently re-

ceived its *Appellation Contrôlée*, and the wines are just beginning to achieve the popularity they deserve.

The district of Alsace, in France's northeastern corner, is another significant wine-producing region. The wines produced in this cool climate are almost exclusively white. Most are made from the Sylvaner, Riesling, and Gewürztraminer grapes, (the region's most successful wines), but some Chardonnays achieve real success in warmer years.

The remaining three important wine regions of France are areas of specialization which are treated separately in this book: Champagne, home of the sparkling wines associated with special occasions, and the two brandy-producing areas of Cognac and Armagnac.

Germany

Germany's wine-producing area is the northernmost in the world. It is also one of the smallest. Germany's wines are light and wonderfully aromatic. Almost all of the exports are white.

The premier white grape is the Riesling. This small slow-ripening grape is sometimes harvested as late as November or December. The two other major grape varieties are the Sylvaner and the Müller-Thurgau. The Sylvaner, cultivated in about one-quarter of the German wine area, produces a mild, fruity wine in greater quantities than the Riesling. Müller-Thurgau is a cross between the Riesling and the Sylvaner.

Some Rulander grapes from vines origi-

Germany

nating in Burgundy are grown. Traminer
and Gewürtztraminer grapes, which tend to
be spicy and fruity, do well throughout the
wine area but only small quantities are harvested.

Germany produces very little red wine
and virtually none is exported. The two
grapes are the *Spätburgunder* (Pinot Noir)
which produces a dark, fruity red wine and
the *Trollinger*, light in color and taste. *Por-
tugieser* is used for the popular domestic
red table wine.

German summers are short and the rare
vintage years generally reflect an unusual
amount of sunshine. Most German vintners
add sugar to the fermenting grape juice to
increase the alcoholic content. This process,
known as *chaptalisation*, is forbidden in the
premium wines, but encouraged for table
wines.

Germany

There are 11 major wine-producing regions in Germany today. Each region has at least two districts made up of several villages, and each village is composed of several vineyards. German wine labels are very specific about these delimited areas.

The Rhinegau, a 20-mile stretch between Wiesbaden and Rüdsheim is the smallest producing area in Germany but one of the most significant. Most of the vineyards are planted with the Riesling grape. This is where the classic sweet, aromatic, and flowery white wines of Germany are produced. The name Johannisberg was assigned to the region when the wine laws were consolidated in 1971. The winery of Schloss Vollrads is one of the finest in the world and is allowed to use its name on the label without additional appellation. Curiously, the nearby town of Assmannshausen produces Germany's best dry red wine from the Pinot Noir grape.

The Rhinehessen region makes a soft, mild wine of the Sylvaner Müller-Thurgau grapes. Rhinehessen is the home of Liebfraumilch, a blended wine that is sold by many producers in the region.

South of Rhinehessen are Rheinpfalz, also known as the Palatinate, and Baden, where a variety of whites are produced. Franken to the east specializes in spicy, dry wines sold in a flagon-shaped bottle. The Mosel-Saar-Ruwer area produces light, gay wines. Mosel comes in a green bottle, Rhine wine in a dark brown.

Three classes of wine come from the 11 wine regions. *Tafelwein* or table wine, which must have an alcoholic content of at least 8.5 percent usually will designate which of the five major river areas the wine comes from. *Qualitätswein* (Q.b.A.) or

Germany

A German wine label

Graf von Schönborn

RHEIN 1975er GAU

Hochheimer Domdechaney
Riesling Spätlese
Qualitätswein mit Prädikat
A. P. Nr. 31.052.018.76
ERZEUGERABFÜLLUNG
Domänenweingut Schloß Schönborn
Shipped by: FREDERICK WILDMAN and SONS Ltd.

quality wine has a higher alcoholic content
and a distinct flavor of the area where they
were produced. *Qualitätswein mit Praedikat*
(Q.m.P) or quality wine with special attri-
butes is the highest rating a German wine
can receive. These wines are allowed to
sweeten naturally on the vine.

These are the five quality classes: **Kabinett**—the grapes were picked at the normal
time around October, no sugar has been
added, and the wine will be elegant and full-
bodied.

Spätlese—the grapes have been allowed
to ripen past the usual harvest time, adding
natural sweetness, body, and flavor. No
sugar can be added. Wines labeled Spätlese
are more expensive than Kabinett.

109

Auslese—the grapes were specially sorted and pressed separately after an extended growth period. Aulese wines tend to be sweeter and more expensive than Spätlese.

Beerenauslese—the wine is made from a combination of ripe and overripe grapes that have begun to develop a mold that eats up the water in the grape, leaving only a drop of very intensely alcoholic liqueur to be pressed out. The mold is called *la pourriture noble* in France and *Edelfäule* in Germany. These wines are rare and very expensive.

Trockenbeerenauslese—made only from grapes that have attained *Edelfäule* state. This wine is incredibly, intensely sweet and is terribly expensive because all the grapes must be sorted by hand. These wines represent German wine-making at its highest.

Eiswein—is made when Trockenbeerenauslese grapes remain on the vine past the first frost. The liquid, once frozen, is transformed into an even more intense flavor. These wines are made only once or twice in a decade.

Italy

The cultural and physical diversity of Italy is reflected in the hundreds, perhaps thousands, of different wines produced throughout the nation.

There are 20 distinct regions and 95 provinces, each with its own distinct production and wines. This broad diversity results in some impressive statistics:

Italy is the largest wine producer in the world.

Italy is the largest wine consumer in the world.

Italy produces more types and varieties of wine than any other nation.

Italy exports more wine to North America (almost 40 million gallons in 1978) than any other country.

Italians and tourists consume more than 80 percent of the country's two-billion-gallon annual output.

Two factors—quality and price—have influenced the exporting of Italian wine.

In 1963, the Italian government took a big step to insure wine quality control by issuing a standard system of classification. Italy's standards are known as the Denominazione di Origine Controllata (D.O.C.) laws. The superior wines meeting these

Italy

strict standards can be depended on for good drinking.

The D.O.C. committee is a jury of wine exporters, grape growers, producers, shippers, state experts, and officials. In addition, the Italian government has encouraged wine science courses and the continuing support and development of the Enoteca Italia, the Italian Wine Institute, which staffs a center in the Medici castle cellar in Siena. It is open to visitors.

Currently there are 204 wines allowed to bear the D.O.C. label. This guarantees that the wine is from the area named, is produced from prescribed proportions of specific grapes by the traditional methods, has been properly aged, and the vintage is valid. Stiff fines are imposed if a misleading label is used.

Before export to North America, a special laboratory check is made by the Italian Trade Institute for clarity and quality. Exported wines receive a Marchio Nazionale label—a red seal with the letters INE.

Categories of D.O.C. wines are as follows:

Simplice—ordinary wines.

Controllata—the classification of the majority of exported wines.

Controllata e garantita—the extraordinary wines that are guaranteed by the government.

Italian wines take their names from the town or district of origin or from a grape variety or both.

The dominant grape for red wine is the hearty Nebbiolo. It is especially impressive in the Piedmont region where the location names of Barolo, Gattinara, Carema, Ghemme, and Barbaresco identify splendid wine. Veneto is the home of Valpolicella and Bardolino.

Italy

BROLIO
CHIANTI CLASSICO
DENOMINAZIONE DI ORIGINE CONTROLLATA
RISERVA

IMBOTTIGLIATO ALL'ORIGINE
NELLE CANTINE DI

DALLA C.V.B. RICASOLI S.p.A.
GAIOLE IN CHIANTI

MARCA DEPOS

PRODUCT OF ITALY

**CASA VINICOLA
BARONE RICASOLI**
FIRENZE - ITALIA

750 ML. (25.4 FL. OZ.)   ALCOHOL 12.7% BY VOL.

IMPORTED BY BROWNE VINTNERS CO.
NEW YORK, N.Y. - S.F. CA.
SOLE DISTRIBUTORS IN THE U.S.A.

An Italian wine label

A grape-plus-place name is Brunello di Montalcino, one of the world's greatest and most expensive wines. Montalcino is located in Tuscany where the Sangiovese grape variety called Brunello produces a wonderful red wine that takes more than 20 years to mature. All the export-quality reds stay in oak casks for a minimum of two years before bottling. Brunello riserva is aged for five years.

Tuscany is also the home of Chianti, Italy's most famous wine. The Chianti district lies between Florence and Siena.

This red wine has been made for over 2,000 years but the blend of grapes that produces the Chianti we know today was developed by Baron Bettino Ricasoli in the nineteenth century. His formula included two red (Sangiovese and Canaiolo) and two white (Malvasia and Trebbiano) grapes. Up to five percent of Chianti may be a blend of local grapes. The grapes are grown only on hilly slopes and must be vinified and aged within the production area.

Young Chianti, which should be drunk within a couple of years, is produced by the "governo all' uso Chianti." It is a blend produced from grapes left to dry on racks to increase their sweetness and mixed with the original wine that was harvested in late September or early October. The mixture is returned to the barrel to ferment another few months until March 1st when Chianti may legally be sold. This produces a light, fresh wine that may have a slight prickle. Aged Chianti doesn't involve the *governo* process. The wine is left in oak barrels for two or three years. If it is aged at least three years at the winery, *riserva* may be added to the label. Bottles are often put down for more than a decade, resulting in a complex and full wine.

Of Chianti's seven D.O.C. geographic areas, Chianti Classico is the best, producing wine of a slightly higher alcoholic content than its neighbors.

Of the increasingly popular Italian white wines, the Verdicchio grape in the Marches region is a good producer. Labels will link it with a town name such as Matellica or Castelli di Jesi. In Umbria, one of the smallest regions, Orvieto produces a popular dry and semi-sweet (*abboccato*) wine. Near Veneto is the small hill district known as Soave. This might be Italy's most famous white wine.

Corvo, a white wine from Sicily, has only recently acquired D.O.C. classification, but has long been popular on American tables.

Portugal

Portugal

Fine wines have been made in Portugal for centuries, but the organization and marketing of the wine industry is still in its infancy. Most likely to be familiar to Americans are the popular roses, of which Mateus and the sparkling Lancer's are the best known. Pleasant as they are for casual drinking, they are far from being the whole story on Portuguese wines.

Portugal produces a number of excellent red wines that age superbly (the best of these have been compared to the great red Burgundies) and some first rate whites. The system of identifying wines, however, can be baffling to outsiders. Some, but not all, fine Portuguese wines are identified by the region of origin, and of those that are, some, but not all, are identified by the vineyard. This is because many wines are made or blended under the supervision of bottling and shipping firms. In effect, the customer relies on the reputation and integrity of the shipper.

The clue to the quality of the contents of the finer bottles is the presence on the label of one of the following terms: *Velho* (old), *Garrafeira* (selected), or *Reserva* (reserved), which is the highest distinction of all).

The finest and oldest Portuguese reds come from Colares in the province of Estorial. The wine region known as Dao (from the Dao river) produces some excellent Reservas and some first rate whites of export quality.

One other group of wines, known as *Vinho Verde* (literally green wine indicating its youth), is of general interest to the wine enthusiast. These fresh, innocent, fruity whites have found favor the world over. The red *Vinhos Verdes* are raw and harsh.

Spain

Spain has the largest acreage under cultivation for wine production of any European country but is only the third largest producer.

The phylloxera epidemic that devastated most of the European vineyards in the late nineteenth century did not hit Spain until the 1930s. The Spanish Civil War and World War II continued the depression in grape production, followed by a series of droughts. Only in the late 1950s did Spanish production begin to pick up. And the government began to oversee quality control in 1970 by instituting a system of *Denominación de Origen* similar to, but without the punitive bite of, the French *Appellation Contrôllée*. There are still many problems with mislabeling by location. Some areas—Rioja in particular—continue a self-policing system. Wine buyers might look for a *Garantia de Origen* on labels which is more reliable.

The largest area of wine production is the broad plain of La Mancha, located southeast of Madrid. Huge amounts of *vino corriente*, Spanish table wine, are produced from the red wine grapes including Cencibel, Monastrel, Tinto Baston, and Gar-

Spain

nacha, the Grenache grape of France. Whites are made from Arien and Jaen. Valdepeñas is probably the best-known area and gives its name to both reds and whites. Most of the Spanish reds tend to be almost black in color, but around Valdepenas the reds (*tintos*) are a clear ruby. The whites (*blancos*) are a pale green or gold.

Although modern vatting and bottling techniques are gradually being implemented, much of the red wine is fermented in *tinajas* or earthenware urns which are 10 feet high and resemble Roman amphorae. Whites and *rosados* (rosés) are racked off sooner than the reds to separate the wine from the grape skins.

A good claret (light red, but not rosé) is made in La Mancha by mixing Cencibel with Arien grapes.

Second in production is Valencia, where the *tintos, clarets,* and *blancos* are heavier and sweeter. Their alcoholic content ranges from 12 to 16 percent. The reds may be drunk after a couple of years in oak casks, where they have already developed a vintage character. Alexis Lichine recommends the red Fondillon but cautions that the supply is small and is usually outstripped by the demand.

Up the coast near Barcelona, the wine areas surrounding Tarragona supply a lot of blending wine that is incorporated into vats in France and Germany. Tarragona used to be known only for its sweet, fortified wines but this is no longer true. The center of its production, the town of Reus, is also known for brilliant, fruity whites. Priorato, a small area within Tarragona, has good, strong (19 to 24 percent alcohol), dry reds.

The entire coastal area of Catalonia is also building up a very good reputation.

Spain

SPAIN

Vines were originally planted in antiquity and during the Middle Ages the wines were much sought after. Today, Torres is the leading table wine and the white wine of Vina Sol is considered exceptional. For the reds, Tres Coronas and Sangre de Toro are recommended.

Carineana is the D.O. applied to the heavier wines of the Aragon province. Dry reds and whites and also sweet versions are produced. Navarre's best wines carry the name of Señiorio de Sarria. Some substantial wines come from Toro, where experts whimsically compare the body of the red wine to the name of the town. Rueda is known for its whites. A particularly interesting winery in the Leon-Castile area is the Vega Sicila. The founder of this little 150-acre place imported wines from Burgundy and Bordeaux. The wines have achieved

119

Spain

considerable reputation in the world market. They are aged in oak barrels for at least five years and the older vintages are labeled *Reserva Especial Unica*.

Throughout Spain, one may find a *vino de pasto* which is a mixture of red and white wine with little or no aging. Wine that has been left in oak for two years or more is labeled *Reserva*. Longer than that rates a *Reserva Especial*.

The premier Spanish wine is Rioja. It was born when Bordeaux vintners fled their phylloxera-destroyed fields in France and crossed the Pyrénées to the lush agricultural land near the Rivers Ebro and Oja. The French brought the fermenting and vatting techniques that are still used today in the nearly 40 bodegas (where wine is made, stored, or drunk). Most wine experts agree that a fine Rioja rivals the wines of Bordeaux and Burgundy.

Rioja is a blended wine made from the Tempranillo (unique to Spain), Garnacha, Graciano, and Mazuelo. Each bodega blends its wines slightly differently. The biggest bodegas might grow most of their own grapes but all of them buy from farmers within the D.O. area of Rioja.

The other secret to Rioja is the years the wine spends in oak barrels. The table wine is aged for at least two years, *Reserva* for four years, and *Gran Reserva* is anything beyond that. The oak mellows the wine and gives it a vanilla-like flavor.

The best Riojas are red. The drier types are marketed in a Bordeaux-type bottle, the fuller, fruitier types in a Burgundy-style flask. But there are Rioja clarets and whites as well. Some wine lovers feel that aging the whites so long in the barrels tends to cook them slightly. These wines could mature in bottles and most wine experts encourage the Rioja producers to get them into glass sooner.

There is some confusion about vintages. Because of the natural evaporation process, some alcohol is lost during the long aging process. Rioja bodegas often top off the barrels with a younger wine. They say that doesn't really change the vintage year, but others may disagree.

The two best bodegas are the Marques de Riscal, founded in 1860, and the Marques de Murietta, both both of whom produce outstanding dry Rioja reds.

Unquestionably the wonderful drinkability of Riojas is enhanced by the price. Bottles are now going for $4.99 for Marques de Riscal red and $2.99 for the white.

Some Rioja bottles are encased in a wire mesh stocking. The practice started when the bodegas tried to eliminate fakes by fixing a wax seal with the bodega stamp on the stocking.

After-dinner Wines

SAUTERNES AND BARSAC Sweet dessert wines reach their peak among the little districts of Sauternes and Barsac, tucked away within the French A.C. area of Graves. The whites produced are big and fragrant. The growers do not harvest at the same time as most vineyards—the grapes are allowed to contract a mold known as *pourriture noble*, or noble rot. As in the making of the German Trockenbeerenauslese, the grapes shrivel into a raisin-like state leaving just one drop of liquid to be pressed. The

After-dinner Wines

mold affects the grapes at different rates, so the vineyard may have as many as eight harvests in one autumn. This golden wine, up to 17 percent alcohol, is made from Sémillon and Sauvignon grapes. It ages well in the bottle and is drinkable for at least 10 years after being laid down.

TOKAY Hungarians use the Sauternes process for the production of Tokay. A percentage of wine from grapes affected by the noble rot is mixed with regular wine. The higher the percentage of the sweet grapes, the richer the wine. Eszencia or Aszu are the names to remember.

MAVRODAPHNE Greece's premier dessert wine is Mavrodaphne, a sweet, heavy red made from the muscat grape in the Peloponnese region.

The muscat is also grown in the United States where sweet dessert wines are made in both California and New York.

PORT Port, the wine of the Upper Douro Valley in northern Portugal, derives its name from the city of Oporto. Although the wine dates back sometime before the Christian era, a trade agreement signed in 1654 between Portugal and England set the stage for the vast British market it has enjoyed for more than three centuries.

More than a dozen different grapes are used in blending port, including Tinta Touriga, Alvarelhao, Souzao, and Bastardo. The vineyards surround Oporto and are called *quintas*. Some shippers now own *quintas* but most of the grapes are still produced on family-owned *quintas* and the harvest is supervised by shippers' representatives.

After-dinner Wines

There are no mechanical devices to separate the grape pips and stems while they are being pressed. Everything goes into the fermenting vat. After about three days, when the fermenting grape juice has reached an alcoholic content of about six or seven percent, a large dose of port brandy is added. This brings the alcoholic content up to about 20 percent while leaving a fairly high sugar level in the wine. It also stops fermentation.

All port is put into wooden casks to age. Vintage port is bottled after two years. A true vintage is declared only three or four times a decade and, although it is usually a unanimous decision by the shippers, occasionally one or two will declare a vintage separately. Once in the bottle, this port will be laid down for 20 or even up to 40 years. A heavy sedimentary deposit, called a crust, develops in the bottle, so great care must be used in decanting port to get the wine out with as little crust as possible.

The other types of port are blends of different vintages. Crusted port is bottled at about four years old, then left to mature in the same way as vintage port. Tawny port is aged in oak for 15 or 20 years. The earlier red color, carefully preserved in vintage or crusted port, fades to a warm golden-brown in the cask. It is ready to drink soon after bottling. Ruby port is aged in oak for up to 10 years. It is a younger, fruiter, and sweeter wine.

Classic port is red or tawny, but the Portuguese drink a white port, which is actually a light gold color, as an aperitif. They have tried to develop an export market for it as the drinking trend has moved to drier and lighter wines, but with little success to date.

123

After-dinner Wines

Port production is controlled by the Instituto do Vinho do Porto in Oporto. The shippers' names, not surprisingly, reflect the British interest in the area and intermarriage with the Portuguese. Some of the most famous are Sandeman, Croft, Ferreira, Taylor, Dow, and Cockburn and Martinez.

Port-type wines are produced in many other areas of the world, including South Africa, Australia, and the United States. They are called port but must include a place of origin on the label.

MADERIA The lighter, drier madeiras are discussed in the aperitif section. Bual and Malmsey are two more that are appropriate after dinner. Bual resembles tawny port as a medium-bodied dessert wine. Malmsey is a heavy, very sweet wine made from the Malvoisie grape.

MARSALA The dark, heavy dessert wine of Sicily is Marsala. The initial wine is made from Catarratto, Grillo, and Inzolia grapes. The final produce reaches an alcoholic level of 18 to 20 percent with the addition of a mixture of brandy and dried grape "must" combined with fresh grape juice that has been reduced almost to a syrup. These elements bring on additional fermentation and give Marsala a distinctive brownish-red tinge. There are four types of Marsala: fini, with an alcoholic content of 17 percent; superiori, aged at least two years in the cask; vergini, commonly made in a solera system where different vintages are blended; and speciali which often has special flavorings, such as strawberries, added. It is thick and sweet.

Spain produces many sweet dessert

After-dinner Wines

wines, both red and white; but the fortified dessert wine is Malaga.

BRANDY Brandy's name comes from a Dutch word that means burnt wine. Almost all wine-producing countries make brandy. It is a simple distillation process of putting the wine over high heat either in a pot still or a continuous still where the liquid is reduced and and alcoholic content raised to upwards of 60 percent. Brandy from local wines is used as a

After-dinner Wines

fortifying agent in sherry, madeira, and port. One of the reasons brandy became a commercial success was because of taxation of liquor throughout European history. Because wine was taxed in bulk, if the amount could be reduced, the tax would be less. The brandy was supposed to be reconstituted with water after it had passed the export-import duties.

The finest brandy is made in France in the Charente region surrounding the town of Cognac. Brandy was produced throughout France in the seventeenth century, but it was the special thin wine of Charente made from Folle Blanche grapes and now mostly St. Émillion grapes, distilled and aged in oak barrels that created the extraordinary brandy known as Cognac.

The wine is made conventionally, then distilled twice in a pot still. The heat vaporizes the wine and as it cools, it is called *brouillis*, a milky liquid with an alcoholic content of about 20 to 30 percent. The *brouillis* is heated again and the first and last portions of the condensation are removed—leaving the heart of about 70 percent alcohol. This is colorless and raw. Limousin oak barrels are prized in Cognac because the absorption of tannin from the wood gives the brandy color and flavor.

The aging process is a variable one that sometimes depends on the economic condition of the manufacturer. The oak barrels are fantastically expensive and the cost of holding the brandy in casks for many years has to be reckoned against the sale price. VSOP Cognac is made of some brandy that has been held in oak for 20 years, but because almost all Cognac is blended, not all of it will have been held that long. VSOP stands for Very Superior Old Pale

After-dinner Wines

but it is something of a misnomer because the color darkens as the wine sits in wood.

Three Star Cognac accounts for about 90 percent of all Cognac sold. The brandy has been aged at least five years. Other designations such as Reserve, X.O., or Cordon Bleu mean that some of the blend has been aged longer than VSOP—but again, the proportion may verge on negligible.

After aging, the brandy is blended, then reduced in alcoholic content by adding a mixture of distilled water and brandy that has had a long rest so the elements can marry. It is poured into bottles that have been rinsed out with Cognac and sealed with a cork that has been dipped in Cognac.

Another name brandy is produced south of Bordeaux in Armagnac. It differs from Cognac in soil and climate and in the distillation process. Armagnac is produced by a continuous still process which means the *brouillis* is not distilled a second time. The brandy is less alcoholic (it cannot exceed 63 percent alcohol) and tends to be less smooth with more distinct flavor and aroma.

The brandy is blended and has the same vintage confusion that Cognac does, but a date on the label means the year of the youngest brandy involved in the blend.

Armagnac oak barrels are required to meet legal appellation; but they, too, are expensive and the supply is dwindling.

In other parts of France, a brandy-type wine called Marc is produced. It is made from the remaining pulp, pits, and stems of earlier pressings for still wine. Two of the most notable are the Marc de Bourgogne and Marc de Champagne.

In Italy, the same process is used to make Grappa, a harsh, young, and functional wine.

Index